Published by
Ulysses Press
P.O. Box 3440
Berkeley, CA 94703
www.ulyssespress.com

ISBN: 978-1-61243-223-6
Library of Congress Catalog Number 2013938280

Printed in China by Everbest through Four Colour Print Group

10 9 8 7 6 5 4 3 2 1

Acquisitions editor: Keith Riegert
Project editor: Alice Riegert
Editor: Susan Lang
Proofreader: Jessica Benner
Layout and design: what!design @ whatweb.com
Photography: © Judi Swinks Photography
Food stylist: Anna Hartman-Kenzler
Illustrator: Karen Bottiani
Index: Sayre Van Young

Distributed by Publishers Group West

to Kevyn Lloyd Aiken

Contents

Introduction   1

Ketchups   9
Fresh Tomato Ketchup   10
Classic Ketchup from Canned Tomatoes   12
Spicy Chipotle Ketchup   13
Tomato–Roasted Red Pepper Ketchup   14
Smoked Tomato Ketchup   16
Spicy Habanero Ketchup   18
Southwestern Tomatillo Ketchup   19
Curried Ketchup   20

Barbecue & Other Essential Sauces   23
Tomato-Based Barbecue Sauce   24
Mustard-Based Barbecue Sauce   25
Whiskey-Spiked Barbecue Sauce   26
Steak Sauce   27
Classic Tartar Sauce   28
Remoulade   29
Red Pepper Coulis   30
Prepared Horseradish Sauce   32
Cocktail Sauce   33

Mustards & Mayonnaises   35
Spicy Smooth Mustard   36
Grainy Porter Mustard   37
Champagne-Dill Mustard   38
Honey Mustard   39

Green Chile Mustard   40
Vidalia Mustard   41
Basic Mayonnaise   42
Sun-Dried Tomato Mayonnaise   44
Chipotle Lime Mayonnaise   45
Classic Aioli   46

Pickles & Relishes   49
Dill Pickles   50
Bread and Butter Pickles   51
Asian Quick Pickles   52
Corn and Pepper Relish   53
Dill Relish   54
Sweet Pickle Relish   55

Hot Sauces & Salsas   57
Tangy Two-Pepper Sauce   58
Rooster-Style Sauce   59
Key Lime–Jalapeño Sauce   60
Mom's Red Chile Sauce   61
Green Chile Sauce   62
Black Bean and Corn Salsa   63
Pico de Gallo   64
Avocado-Tomatillo Salsa   65
Tropical Salsa   66

Infused Oils & Vinegars   69
Roasted Garlic Olive Oil   70
Rosemary-Infused Oil   71

Lemon-Infused Oil 72
Fig-Infused Vinegar 73
Raspberry Vinegar 74
Herbed Balsamic Vinegar 75

Salad Dressings 77

Classic Vinaigrette 78
Maple Tarragon Vinaigrette 79
Dilly Ranch Dressing 80
Lemon Poppy Seed Buttermilk Dressing 81
Lime-Cumin Dressing 82
Sesame-Ginger Dressing 83
Avocado Goddess Dressing 84
Caesar Dressing 85
Blue Cheese Dressing 86
Orange-Miso Dressing 87

Ethnic & Specialty Condiments 89

Sweet Chili Sauce 90
Apricot Sweet and Sour Sauce 91
Tapenade 92
Chimichurri 93
Cilantro-Almond Pesto 94
Red Pepper Preserves 95
Teriyaki Sauce 96
Hoisin Sauce 97
Caramelized Onion Chutney 98
Pear Chutney 99
Mango Chutney 100

Bacon Jam 101

Sweet Sauces & Spreads 103

Peanut Butter 104
Almond Butter 105
Chocolate Almond Spread 106
Hot Fudge Sauce 107
Caramel Sauce 108
Berry Sauce 109
Crunchy-Shell Chocolate Sauce 110
Dulce de Leche 111
Wet Walnuts 112
Luscious Lemon Curd 113
Cherry-Fig Compote 114
Tropical Pineapple-Cashew Compote 115

Appendix 116

Food Safety and Canning 116
Condiments as Gifts 120

Resources 122

Conversion Charts 123

Index 124

About the Author 129

Introduction

"Condiments are like old friends—highly thought of, but often taken for granted," once quipped Marilyn Kaytor, one of America's first true food journalists.

Stop for a moment and think about a world without condiments: would a hot dog be as delicious without its blanket of ketchup, mustard, and relish? How sad would a salad be without a drizzle of dressing? Bread would be dry and dull without a slathering of jam, and even the most delicious ice cream is all the better when it's topped with hot fudge or caramel sauce.

If you've picked up this book, chances are you have a refrigerator door full of bottles of mustard, mayonnaise, pickles, and other condiments, and you're wondering if there are better options than the mass-produced, commercial brands on the supermarket shelves.

Indeed, there are. On the pages of this book you'll find true alchemy: how to break down a basket of ripe tomatoes from your garden into a jar of ruby-red ketchup. How to whip up the perfect salad dressing to complement tonight's dinner, all with ingredients you already have in your pantry. How to custom-blend a hot sauce so that it's just spicy enough for your palate.

Stick with me, and you might never have to buy another bottle of commercially prepared condiment again.

Why Make Your Own?

As you'll learn on the following pages, making your own condiments is easy and fun. And there are many advantages to making condiments yourself instead of purchasing them.

You'll know exactly what goes into each batch. Many commercial condiments like ketchup, dressings, and hot sauces contain high fructose corn syrup, artificial flavorings, preservatives, MSG, and other undesirable ingredients. And who knows what the generic term "natural flavorings," so often included in the list of ingredients, means?

You can use fresh, locally grown and natural or organic ingredients. Many of the recipes in this book can be made with herbs, fruits, and vegetables grown in your own backyard or bought at a farmer's market or natural food store. Not only are homemade condiments a great way to make use of seasonal bounty, but they'll be fresher and, in many cases, healthier than store-bought versions.

You can customize your condiments according to your palate and your needs. Make a sauce spicier or milder, reduce the amount of oil or salt in a salad dressing to be a little healthier, or alter a tartar sauce recipe to complement the type of fish you're cooking.

It's fun! There is no small satisfaction in taking fresh produce and seeing the magic unfold as it transforms into a flavorful condiment. It's particularly exciting for small children to learn exactly where their food comes from. My children loved watching pounds and pounds of fresh tomatoes morph into a jar of ketchup.

Homemade condiments make wonderful gifts. Use one of the recipes in this book to create your own condiments, package them in gorgeous jars or bottles, create fun custom labels, and give them as gifts. They make fantastic stocking stuffers, hostess gifts, or even party or wedding favors.

Condiments: A Brief History

I like to imagine a cave man biting into his woolly mammoth steak and imagining that a little dash of spice might jazz it up. And indeed early condiments like salt, pepper, and herbs, were likely used as a way to add interest to bland, monotonous foods at a time when there was little variety in what humans ate.

According to *The Oxford Companion to American Food and Drink*, condiments have been in use in America since colonial times and were at first on the tables of only those who could afford them. Most common were jams and jellies, mustards, salt, and pepper. Early American housewives soon learned to "put up" pickled vegetables, jams, and other produce-based canned foods for the long winter, and jars of these foods would sustain them until the spring, when they could once again grow or forage for fresh fruits and vegetables.

By the 19th century, condiments would become a matter of controversy: activists spoke out against condiments. Dietary reformer Sylvester Graham accused them of being "highly exciting and exhausting," while physician and temperance leader Dio Lewis encouraged his followers to shun mustard, ketchup, and other flavor enhancers, railing, "Everything which inflames one appetite is likely to arouse the other also."

Luckily for us, Americans had already developed an appetite for condiments, and their popularity has grown ever since, particularly as ingredients and manufacturing processes became less expensive. The emergence of fast food in the middle of the 20th century helped spur the popularity of ketchup, mustard, and mayonnaise, and the accessibility of different cultures, through travel, the media, and immigrant populations increased the presence of international ingredients and condiments available to us in American supermarkets and restaurants.

Setting Up Your Pantry

Keeping a number of staples on hand, and having access to fresh, good-quality produce, will ensure that you will always be ready to make your own condiments.

The Staples

Vinegars: Many of the condiments in this book require the use of different varieties of vinegar. Not only does vinegar add a flavorful acidic note to a condiment, but it also acts as a natural preservative. The acetic acid in vinegar (commercially available vinegars contain between 4 and 7 percent acidity) can inhibit the growth of many microbes, molds, and bacteria (which is why vinegar can double as a homegrown cleaning solution). Vinegar can be made from any fruit or anything containing sugar (typically fruits or grains), but there are certain kinds of vinegar that are most frequently used in this book. White vinegar is the least expensive and most common vinegar, and it's one of the purest forms of acetic acid; it's derived from pure alcohol and has a very straightforward, simple flavor. Cider vinegar, which is yeast-fermented apple juice, has a fruity, sweet-tart flavor that works nicely in certain ketchup and mustard recipes, and in hot sauces. Wine vinegar is made from a twofold fermentation of grape juice and can be found in either white or red varieties. Sherry vinegar, champagne vinegar, and balsamic vinegar are all varieties of wine vinegar. These types of vinegars are particularly nice in salad dressings. Other vinegar varieties include malt vinegar (derived from malt, or sprouted grain) and rice vinegar (made from sugar derived from rice). A traditional Asian ingredient, rice vinegar has a very mild, almost floral flavor. Be sure to buy plain rice vinegar and not the seasoned kind, which contains sugar. Because of its acidity, vinegar will last indefinitely and doesn't need refrigeration.

Dried Herbs and Spices: Many of the recipes in this book are seasoned with spices or dried herbs, which can, say, add complexity to a ketchup, give a new personality to mayonnaise, or add interest to salad dressing. My favorite source for dried herbs and spices is a popular local natural food store that sells them in bulk. Because it's such a busy store, I know that the bulk spice section gets replenished regularly, and I like that I can buy as much (or as little) as I wish. It's an economical way to shop for herbs, and you can buy just what you need so that the remainder doesn't languish in your pantry. Dried herbs and spices will begin to lose their potency after 6 months or so and, although using them past their prime isn't likely to make you sick, they won't contribute much flavor to your recipe. A good way to tell if your herbs and spices are still fresh is to give them a sniff—if they're still pungent, chances are they have flavor left in them. You can also order in bulk online (try bulkfoods.com).

Fruits and Vegetables: Originally, the term "condiment" referred to pickled or preserved foods, according to *The Oxford Companion to American Food and Drink*. Indeed, creating condiments is a wonderful way to use and preserve fresh fruits, vegetables, and herbs from your own garden, purchased at a farmer's market, or simply from the produce department in your supermarket. In some instances, the nice thing about these condiment recipes is that the produce doesn't have to be flawless. You can use bruised fruit to make jams, and the tomatoes in ketchup recipes simmer down so much that you can even used ones that are beginning to get a little mushy. If you plan on making large batches of condiments, see if your city has a large commercial produce market that's open to the public. Usually these markets, where smaller restaurants and grocers shop, have super fresh produce at very reasonable prices.

Canned vs. Frozen: For some of the recipes in this book, you can use canned or frozen versions of fruits and vegetables. For instance, canned tomatoes can be used in ketchups. I prefer to buy imported or organic brands (Muir Glen is one of my favorites) as they are less likely to have BPA, a potentially toxic chemical, in the interior coating of their cans, and they're usually much lower in sodium than mainstream brands. When it comes to fruit for sauces and jams, frozen is a far better choice than canned. The fruit is typically picked at its peak and frozen immediately after picking, so it retains its flavor and nutrients. Plus, there's nothing added to it in the way of salt, preservatives, or sugary syrup.

Fresh Herbs: Many of the recipes in this book rely on herbs for flavor. Choose herbs with leaves that look fresh and unwilted. You can extend the life of cut basil, parsley, and cilantro by storing them in the refrigerator with their stems in a cup of water, like flowers in a vase. Herbs can also be kept loosely wrapped in a damp paper towel, in a plastic bag in the refrigerator. Even better: Grow your own in pots on a sunny windowsill.

A Well-Equipped Kitchen

Certain kitchen tools will help you be more successful in making condiments. Here are some recommendations for outfitting your kitchen with the right tools.

Cookware: For cooked sauces like jam, ketchup, and barbecue sauce I like heavy-bottom saucepans ranging in size from 1 to 3 quarts, depending on how large a batch you're making. Whether it's uncoated stainless steel or nonstick is up to you. Nonstick finishes will make cleanup easier, but keep in mind that the finish can easily become scratched or chipped, so be sure not to use metal whisks or other sharp, hard utensils with the pan. Instead, use wooden spoons and silicone-coated whisks and spatulas. Whatever pans you choose, the best ones are heavy and thick and preferably made of stainless steel, which conducts and retains heat well (an aluminum or copper core is a bonus, as it helps with conductivity of the heat). For making large batches of cooked condiments and for jam, an enameled cast-iron Dutch oven—from Le Creuset, for example—is a good choice.

Food Mill: A food mill is like a strainer with a paddle on a crank. When you turn the crank, the paddle sweeps along the surface of the strainer, pushing the food against the holes and forcing it through while keeping undesirable solids out of the sauce. It's great for applesauce, ketchup, tomato sauce, coulis, and other smooth concoctions. Look for a food mill with several different discs that will create fine, medium, and coarse textures.

Whisks: I like having both large and small whisks on hand. A small whisk is a good size for small batches of sauces or for making salad dressing, while a larger whisk is helpful for stirring a pan full of ingredients. With a nonstick pan, be sure to use a silicone-coated whisk so it won't scratch the finish.

Mixing Bowls: A set of mixing bowls in a wide variety of sizes is great for prepping and combining ingredients. My two favorite materials are metal and glass. Metal bowls are lightweight, super durable, and heat resistant, although they will move around on the countertop if you're whisking vigorously (try anchoring them on a damp towel twisted into a ring shape). Tempered glass bowls have a nice heft to them and are heatproof and nonreactive. A metal or glass bowl can stand in for a double boiler insert by fitting it inside a saucepan containing an inch or two of water (the bottom of the bowl should not make contact with the water).

Measuring Utensils: You'll get the best results by precisely measuring all the ingredients, at least until you become more familiar with the recipes and want to play around with increasing or decreasing seasonings, sweeteners, and other ingredients. I love stainless steel dry-ingredient measuring cups because they're durable and sit sturdily on the counter as you're spooning ingredients into them. And there are double-ended measuring spoons, ideal when you need the same quantity of two different spices and don't want to have to rinse and dry your spoon between each scoop, or for when you're measuring the same quantity in both liquid and dry ingredients (Progressive International makes a great set with magnets imbedded in the handles to hold the spoons nested neatly together in the drawer). Be sure you have liquid measuring utensils as well. I like a 2-cup liquid measuring cup as well as a mini measuring beaker that measures in tablespoons and ounces.

Funnel: A plastic or metal funnel is good for pouring sauces into bottles and jars. Look for one that is heat safe. Funnels with small openings are ideal for pouring liquids into bottles, while you can find special canning funnels, which have wider openings, to fill canning jars.

Food Processor or Blender: A food processor or a blender can quickly chop or puree ingredients for salsas and can also make mayonnaise and salad dressings. Of the two, a food processor is more versatile as many come with shredding and slicing disks for vegetables or cheese. You might also find a mini food processor to be handy for processing the smaller-sized batches that many of these recipes make. Mini food processors usually have a 4-cup capacity work bowl. An immersion blender can also be helpful for pureeing ingredients directly in a bowl or a pan.

Cutlery: The three most essential knives in any kitchen, but especially for the recipes in this book, are a chef's knife, a paring or utility knife, and a serrated knife. The chef's knife will be your most-used knife; its long blade can handle any task, from chopping onions to mincing a handful of herbs. The paring or utility knife, which has a shorter blade (my favorite is a utility knife with a 4-inch blade) is wonderful for small-scale jobs like coring tomatoes, cutting up avocados, hulling strawberries, mincing garlic or shallots, peeling apples, and cutting citrus. And the serrated knife can slice tomatoes, peaches, and other soft and delicate produce without bruising it. It's also useful for slicing bread. When shopping for cutlery, the brand and design is a personal decision based on what feels good in your hand, so shop at a store where you can actually pick up the knives and mimic a cutting motion. Higher-end cutlery brands will likely have forged blades (where molten metal is poured into a mold to form the blade, and then the shape and blade are hand finished), while less pricey brands have stamped blades, which are cut from a sheet of metal. On the high end, I love Shun and Wüsthof Trident knives, while Victorinox makes a more economical line of fantastic knives that are comfortable to hold and retain their sharp edge.

Cutting Boards: Choose wood, bamboo, or wood fiber-and-resin cutting boards (such as Epicurean cutting boards), none of which will dull a knife. For creating the condiments in this book, I suggest investing in two cutting boards and delegating one for fruits and other sweet ingredients, and the other for strong-flavored ingredients like onions, garlic, and chiles. After all, there's nothing worse than making a sweet fruit sauce that tastes faintly of garlic!

Tasting Spoons: As you work through the recipes in this book, you'll do a lot of sampling to check the thickness of a sauce and to adjust seasonings, or simply to admire your handiwork! While there's nothing wrong with using everyday spoons for sampling, I have a few designated tasting spoons that I use specifically for tasting food as I cook. My favorite is a long-handled stainless steel bar spoon, which is long enough to reach into a deep pot. Find a tasting spoon you like and keep a few on hand, because of course you'll want to wash a spoon between tastes.

Disposable Gloves: If you've ever rubbed your eyes after you've handled spicy chile peppers, you'll understand why it's wise to have a packet of disposable food-handling gloves on hand. Available at restaurant supply stores and online, they can protect your hands while you're handling spicy ingredients. If you're finicky and don't want the lingering odor of onions or garlic on your hands, you can use the gloves to work with any pungent ingredients.

Kitchen Scale: Many of the ingredients in this book, particularly fruits and vegetables, are listed by weight to ensure more consistent recipes. A scale is indeed a handy tool to more precisely measure ingredients and to portion out the finished product into batches. I find digital scales to be more compact and easier to use than analog versions; look for one that will measure in gradations of a fraction of an ounce.

Ketchups

Savory, tomato-based sauces like ketchups and barbecue sauces are among the most prevalent and popular condiments. More than 90 percent of Americans put ketchup on their burgers when they're eating them in a restaurant, found one study. But ketchup as we know it actually has its origins in Southeast Asia as a fermented sauce made from soybeans, according to *The Oxford Companion to American Food and Drink*. British explorers brought the sauce home from their travels, and it eventually made its way to America by way of colonists. Tomato ketchup, however, is likely an invention of Americans, and it is believed to have been used and bottled as early as the early 19th century.

Making ketchup from scratch is surprisingly easy, if time consuming (although most of the time is largely hands-off). You'll be rewarded for your efforts by a fresh-tasting, thick condiment that is every bit as versatile as the bottled stuff—and better for you, since you're guaranteed that it's free of high fructose corn syrup and preservatives.

Fresh Tomato Ketchup

If you have a surplus of tomatoes from your garden, making homemade ketchup is a wonderful way to capture and preserve their bright, summery flavor. It's a project that takes most of the afternoon, but you'll be rewarded with a ketchup that's far more vibrantly flavored than store-bought ketchup and not so syrupy-sweet. The best tomatoes to use for this are plum or paste tomatoes, but any tomato will work. Because the tomatoes reduce so much, I found that even tomatoes that aren't super flavorful still made an incredibly tasty ketchup.

Makes 12 ounces

6 pounds plum tomatoes

$\frac{2}{3}$ cup cider vinegar

$\frac{2}{3}$ cup chopped yellow onion (about 1 medium)

$\frac{1}{4}$ cup brown sugar

1 teaspoon celery seeds

$\frac{1}{4}$ teaspoon ground cinnamon

$\frac{1}{4}$ teaspoon ground allspice

$\frac{1}{8}$ teaspoon ground cloves

$\frac{1}{4}$ teaspoon kosher salt

Bring a large pot of water to a boil and fill a large bowl with ice and cold water. While the water is heating, prepare the tomatoes by using a paring knife to cut out the cores and cut an X in the skin on the bottom of each. Working in batches if necessary, immerse the tomatoes in the boiling water for 1 minute, then immediately plunge them in the ice water for 1 minute. When the tomatoes are cool enough to handle, peel the skin—it should come right off. Quarter the tomatoes and use your fingers to scoop out and discard the seeds and pulp.

Place the tomatoes in a large saucepan and add the cider vinegar, onion, brown sugar, and celery seeds. Bring to a simmer over medium heat, then reduce the heat to medium-low and simmer, uncovered, stirring occasionally, until the tomato mixture is reduced to about one quarter of its original volume, about 2 to 2$\frac{1}{2}$ hours. Remove from the heat, and let cool for 10 to 15 minutes.

Use It For
• Topping for hot dogs and hamburgers.
• Adding to meatloaf mixture, or brushing on top as a glaze before cooking.
• Stirring together with mayonnaise to make a special sauce for burgers.
• Dipping sauce for french fries or onion rings.
• Stirring into cottage cheese.

Place a food mill fitted with a medium disc over a large bowl and pass the tomato mixture through the mill. Discard the solids that don't pass through the sieve. Transfer the tomato liquid into a clean saucepan over medium heat. Stir in the cinnamon, allspice, cloves, and salt. Bring to a simmer over medium heat, then reduce the heat to low and let simmer, uncovered and stirring occasionally, for 30 minutes to 1 hour, until reduced by half and very thick and dark red. Let cool, then spoon into sterilized glass jars. The ketchup will keep in the refrigerator for up to 4 weeks.

Classic Ketchup from Canned Tomatoes

When fresh tomatoes are out of season, canned tomatoes are great for making ketchup. The end result will have a richer tomato flavor and possibly a darker color, since canned tomatoes are a little more concentrated than fresh, and it might take less time to cook than if you were to use fresh tomatoes. I prefer canned whole tomatoes, either organic brands or ones imported from Italy.

Makes about 15 ounces

2 (28-ounce) cans whole peeled tomatoes	¼ cup cider vinegar	¼ teaspoon cinnamon
½ cup chopped yellow onion (about 1 small)	2 tablespoons brown sugar	⅛ teaspoon ground cloves
	½ teaspoon celery seeds	¼ teaspoon kosher salt
	¼ teaspoon ground allspice	

In a large saucepan, combine the tomatoes, onion, vinegar, brown sugar, and celery seeds. Bring to a simmer over medium heat, then reduce the heat to medium-low and let simmer, uncovered, about 2 hours, stirring occasionally and using a spoon to break up the tomato pieces, until the mixture has reduced by roughly half and the tomato pieces are falling apart. Remove from the heat and let cool for 10 to 15 minutes.

Place a food mill fitted with a medium disc over a large bowl. Pass the tomato mixture through the food mill, discarding solids that don't fit through the sieve. Return the tomato liquid in the bowl to a clean saucepan over medium heat. Stir in the allspice, cinnamon, cloves, and salt. Bring to a simmer, then reduce the heat to low to maintain the simmer. Simmer, uncovered and stirring occasionally, for about 1 hour, or until thickened and reduced. Let cool, then spoon into sterilized glass jars. The ketchup will keep in the refrigerator for up to 4 weeks.

Use It For

- In place of tomato paste in pasta or pizza sauce.
- Topping for hot dogs and hamburgers.
- Base for barbecue sauce.
- Stir into Asian noodle dishes with a sweet-and-sour flavor profile, such as pad Thai.
- Mix with horseradish and lemon juice for cocktail sauce.

Spicy Chipotle Ketchup

Canned or dried chipotle chiles (smoked jalapeños) give this ketchup its lively kick. To tone it down, use just one chipotle. When using dried chiles, reconstitute them in ½ cup boiling water for 10 to 15 minutes. If you prefer fresh tomatoes, you'll need 4 pounds and you'll have to core, peel, and seed them (see page 10). They might need to cook a bit longer than canned tomatoes.

Makes about 15 ounces

2 (28-ounce) cans whole peeled tomatoes	2 canned chipotle chile peppers in adobo sauce, seeds removed, roughly chopped	½ teaspoon ground cumin
½ cup chopped yellow onion (about 1 small)		¼ teaspoon cinnamon
¼ cup white vinegar	1 tablespoon brown sugar	⅛ teaspoon kosher salt
	½ teaspoon celery seeds	

In a large saucepan, combine the tomatoes, onion, vinegar, chiles, brown sugar, and celery seeds. Bring to a simmer over medium heat, then reduce the heat to medium-low and let simmer, uncovered, about 2 hours, stirring occasionally and using a spoon to break up the tomato pieces, until the mixture has reduced by roughly half and the tomato pieces are falling apart. Remove from the heat and let cool for 10 to 15 minutes.

Place a food mill fitted with a medium disc over a large bowl. Pass the tomato mixture through the mill, discarding any solids that are caught. Return the pureed mixture to a clean saucepan over medium heat. Stir in the cumin, cinnamon, and salt. Bring to a simmer, then reduce the heat to low to maintain the simmer. Simmer, uncovered, stirring occasionally, for about 1 hour, or until thickened and reduced by half. The ketchup will keep in the refrigerator for up to 4 weeks.

Use It For
- Make a Southwestern-style meatloaf.
- Turkey burger topping along with sliced avocado and sprouts.
- Stir a spoonful into a Bloody Mary for depth of flavor and spice.
- Spread on chicken before baking.
- Stir into ground beef for spicy sloppy joes.

Tomato–Roasted Red Pepper Ketchup

Roasted red peppers add a depth and richness to ketchup. In this recipe, the peppers are roasted in the oven's broiler, but you could roast them on a gas or charcoal grill, or over a gas burner. You'll get the best results if you look for peppers that are round and uniform in size rather than ones that are oddly shaped.

Makes 6 to 8 ounces

1 pound red bell peppers (about 3 medium)

2 pounds plum tomatoes

1/3 cup white vinegar or cider vinegar

2 tablespoons brown sugar

1 teaspoon celery seeds

1/8 teaspoon ground cinnamon

1/8 teaspoon ground cloves

1/4 teaspoon kosher salt

Preheat the broiler. Place the peppers on a baking sheet and set on an oven rack positioned so the peppers are about 4 to 6 inches from the broiler. Turn the peppers with tongs so that all sides are evenly blackened and blistered, about 15 to 20 minutes. Place immediately in a heatproof bowl and cover tightly with plastic wrap. Let sit for 15 minutes, until cooled. Use your fingers to peel and rub the skin off. Remove the stems, seeds, and membranes. Roughly chop the peppers.

While the peppers are broiling and cooling, bring a large pot of water to a boil and fill a large bowl with ice and cold water. While the water is heating, prepare the tomatoes by using a paring knife to cut out the cores and cut an X in the skin on the bottom of each. Working in batches if necessary, immerse the tomatoes in the boiling water for 1 minute, then immediately plunge them into the ice water for 1 minute. When the tomatoes

Use It For

- Brush on meatloaf before cooking for a tangy-sweet glaze.
- Turkey burger topping, along with smoked gouda and a few leaves of romaine.
- Stir a dollop into tomato soup for added flavor.
- Mix with equal parts mayo for a sandwich spread.
- Dipping sauce for steak fries or Tater Tots.

are cool enough to handle, peel the skin—it should come right off. Quarter the tomatoes and use your fingers to scoop out the seeds and pulp.

Place the tomatoes and roasted peppers in a large saucepan and add the vinegar, brown sugar, and celery seeds. Bring to a simmer over medium heat, then reduce the heat to medium-low and simmer, uncovered, stirring occasionally and breaking the chunks apart with a spoon, until the mixture has reduced to one quarter or one third of its original volume, about 2 hours. Remove from the heat, and let cool for 10 to 15 minutes.

Place a food mill fitted with a medium disc over a large bowl and pass the tomato mixture through the mill. Discard the solids that don't pass through the sieve. Transfer the mixture to a clean saucepan over medium heat. Add the cinnamon, cloves, and salt. Bring to a simmer over medium heat, then reduce the heat to low and let simmer, uncovered and stirring occasionally, for 1 hour or more, until the sauce is very thick and dark red. Let cool, then spoon into sterilized glass jars. The ketchup will keep in the refrigerator for up to 4 weeks.

Smoked Tomato Ketchup

This recipe uses a stovetop smoker to infuse fresh tomatoes with a deep, smoky flavor. Stovetop smokers can be found at kitchenware stores for less than $50 and are great for smoking fish and meats right on your stove. If you don't have a smoker, you can smoke the tomatoes on your outdoor grill by adding wood chips to the grill. I like hickory chips for the most distinctive smoky flavor.

Makes 4 ounces

2 pounds plum tomatoes	¼ cup cider vinegar	⅛ teaspoon ground cinnamon
1 tablespoon hickory woodchips, for smoking	½ teaspoon celery seeds	⅛ teaspoon ground allspice
¼ cup minced shallot (about 1 medium)	2 tablespoons plus 1 ½ teaspoons brown sugar, divided	¼ teaspoon kosher salt

Bring a large pot of water to a boil and fill a large bowl with ice and cold water. While the water is heating, prepare the tomatoes by using a paring knife to cut out the cores, and cut an X in the skin on the bottom of each. Working in batches if necessary, immerse the tomatoes in the boiling water for 1 minute, then immediately plunge them into the ice water for 1 minute. When the tomatoes are cool enough to handle, peel the skin—it should come right off. Quarter the tomatoes and use your fingers to scoop out the seeds and pulp.

To smoke the tomatoes, place the hickory chips in the bottom of a stovetop smoker, then cover with the drip tray and food rack. Arrange the tomatoes in a single layer on the rack. Cover and cook over medium-low heat for about 15 minutes. Remove from the heat, and let rest about 5 minutes. Transfer the tomatoes to a saucepan and add the

Use It For
- Base for barbecue sauce.
- Topping for bratwurst or Italian sausage.
- Add horseradish and use as a dipping sauce for grilled shrimp.
- Brush on pork before grilling.
- Mix with cooked ground beef for sloppy joes.

shallot, vinegar, celery seeds, and 2 tablespoons brown sugar. Simmer uncovered for about 2 hours, stirring occasionally and breaking up the tomatoes with a spoon, until the sauce has thickened and reduced. Let cool for about 10 minutes, then pass through a food mill fitted with a medium disc and set over a bowl. Discard any solids that are caught.

Return the pureed mixture to a clean saucepan, add the cinnamon, allspice, salt, and remaining 1 ½ teaspoons brown sugar. Bring to a simmer over medium heat, then reduce the heat to low and let simmer, uncovered and stirring occasionally, for 30 minutes to 1 hour, until reduced by half and very thick and dark red. Let cool, then spoon into sterilized glass jars. The ketchup will keep in the refrigerator for up to 4 weeks.

Spicy Habanero Ketchup

A habanero's tiny size is deceptive: the little lantern-shaped chiles pack a punch, which is why this recipe only calls for 1. Wear food-handling gloves while you're working with the chiles.

Makes 12 ounces

4 pounds plum tomatoes	2 tablespoons brown sugar	1 teaspoon ground cumin
¼ cup cider vinegar	1 habanero chile pepper, seeds and membranes removed, roughly chopped	¼ teaspoon ground cinnamon
¼ cup chopped yellow onion (about ½ small)		¼ teaspoon ground allspice
	1 teaspoon celery seeds	¼ teaspoon kosher salt

Bring a large pot of water to a boil and fill a large bowl with ice and cold water. While the water is heating, prepare the tomatoes by using a paring knife to cut out the cores and cut an X in the skin on the bottom of each. Working in batches if necessary, immerse the tomatoes in the boiling water for 1 minute, then immediately plunge them into the ice water for 1 minute. When the tomatoes are cool enough to handle, use your fingers to peel the skin. Quarter the tomatoes and use your fingers to scoop out the seeds and pulp.

Place the tomatoes in a large saucepan and add the vinegar, onion, brown sugar, habanero, and celery seeds. Bring to a simmer over medium heat, then reduce the heat to medium-low and simmer, uncovered, stirring occasionally, until the tomato mixture is reduced to about one-quarter of its original volume, about 2 to 2½ hours. Remove from the heat and let cool for 10 to 15 minutes.

Place a food mill fitted with a medium disc over a large bowl and pass the tomato mixture through the mill. Discard the solids that don't pass through the sieve. Transfer the pureed mixture to a clean saucepan over medium heat. Add the cumin, cinnamon, allspice, and salt. Bring to a simmer over medium heat, then reduce the heat to low and let simmer, uncovered, stirring occasionally, for 30 minutes to 1 hour, until reduced by half and very thick and dark red. Let cool, then spoon into sterilized glass jars. The ketchup will keep in the refrigerator for up to 4 weeks.

Use It For
- On turkey dogs along with relish and diced avocado.
- In a baked beans recipe.
- Brush on pork chops or lamb chops before grilling.

Southwestern Tomatillo Ketchup

Tomatillos look like tiny green tomatoes (except that they're covered in a papery husk), so it makes sense that they'd make one heck of a ketchup. This is one of my favorite ketchup recipes: I love how the normally very tart tomatillos mellow with the long cooking time, and the finished ketchup has a jammy, spreadable consistency.

Makes 6 to 8 ounces

2 pounds tomatillos	2 medium cloves garlic, minced	2 tablespoons lime juice
$\frac{1}{4}$ cup brown sugar	1 teaspoon ground cumin	$\frac{1}{4}$ teaspoon kosher salt
$\frac{1}{4}$ cup rice vinegar	1 tablespoon fresh minced cilantro	$\frac{1}{4}$ teaspoon ground cinnamon

To prepare the tomatillos, remove the papery husks and stems, rinse off the sticky residue, and quarter them. Place the tomatillos along with the brown sugar, vinegar, and garlic in a medium saucepan. Simmer, uncovered, for about 2 hours over medium-low heat, stirring occasionally and breaking up the chunks with a spoon, until the tomatillos are mostly broken down and the mixture is very thick and reduced. Let cool for about 10 minutes, then pass through a food mill fitted with the finest disc and set over a bowl. Discard any solids that are caught.

Return the pureed mixture to a clean saucepan, and add the cumin, cilantro, lime juice, salt, and cinnamon. Simmer, uncovered and stirring occasionally for 30 minutes, until very thick, then transfer the mixture to a sterilized jar. The ketchup will keep in the refrigerator for up to 4 weeks.

Use It For

- Spread a layer on the inside of a quesadilla.
- Dipping sauce for sweet potato fries.
- Slather on a Southwestern-style hot dog, along with green chiles, diced avocado, and pepper jack cheese.
- Spread on salmon before grilling.
- Topping for grilled shrimp tacos.

Curried Ketchup

The addition of curry gives ketchup a warmth and touch of exoticism that can dress up anything from a plain old burger to more international fare. It's a particularly popular condiment in Germany and Belgium and is the basis for Germany's sausage dish currywurst. If you want to use canned tomatoes instead of fresh, you'll need two 28-ounce cans of whole peeled tomatoes.

Makes 12 ounces

4 pounds plum tomatoes	2 tablespoons brown sugar	¼ teaspoon ground allspice
¼ cup red wine vinegar	1 teaspoon celery seeds	⅛ teaspoon ground cloves
¼ cup minced shallot (about 1 medium)	2 teaspoons curry powder	¼ teaspoon kosher salt
	¼ teaspoon ground cinnamon	

Bring a large pot of water to a boil and fill a large bowl with ice and cold water. While the water is heating, prepare the tomatoes by using a paring knife to cut out the cores and cut an X in the skin on the bottom of each. Working in batches if necessary, immerse the tomatoes in the boiling water for 1 minute, then immediately plunge them into the ice water for 1 minute. When the tomatoes are cool enough to handle, peel the skin—it should come right off. Quarter the tomatoes and use your fingers to scoop out the seeds and pulp.

Place the tomatoes in a large saucepan and add the vinegar, shallot, brown sugar, celery seeds, and curry powder. Bring to a simmer over medium heat, then reduce the heat to medium-low and simmer, uncovered, stirring occasionally, until the tomato mixture is reduced to about one-quarter of its original volume, about 2 to 2½ hours. Remove from the heat, and let cool for 10 to 15 minutes.

Place a food mill fitted with a medium disc over a large bowl and pass the tomato mixture through the mill. Discard the solids that don't pass through the sieve. Transfer the pureed mixture to a clean

Use It For
- Heat and serve over sliced German pork sausage (currywurst).
- Dipping sauce for french fries or sweet potato fries.
- Dipping sauce for samosas.
- Mix with yogurt for a creamy sauce for cooked chicken or pork.
- Hamburger topping along with mango chutney, goat cheese, and pickled onions.

saucepan over medium heat. Add the cinnamon, allspice, ground cloves, and salt. Bring to a simmer over medium heat, then reduce the heat to low and let simmer, uncovered and stirring occasionally, for 30 minutes to 1 hour, until reduced by half and very thick and dark red. Let cool, then spoon into sterilized glass jars. The ketchup will keep in the refrigerator for up to 4 weeks.

Barbecue & Other Essential Sauces

Barbecue sauce has become a fiercely contested and defended topic in various parts of the United States, from the Carolinas to Texas. Different regions have specific methods of cooking and seasoning their meat, and you'll find that the toppings for these meats vary widely as well. Like ketchup, pit barbecue is a culinary tradition that dates back to the colonists and has evolved across the country as different nationalities settled in various regions. In many cases, the sauce is simply a handful of ingredients and seasonings (often condiments themselves) combined and simmered together.

The other condiments in this chapter are a wonderful way to accentuate a piece of fish, meat, or chicken, whether it's roasted, sautéed, grilled, or braised. For the most part, these condiments are easy to mix together while the meat is cooking, and they add an element of complexity as well as a fancy, restaurant-caliber touch.

Tomato-Based Barbecue Sauce

Sweet and tangy, ketchup-based barbecue sauces reign in Kansas City, Memphis, and St. Louis. As a Midwesterner by birth, I think of this type of sauce as the quintessential barbecue sauce. This version has a kick thanks to chipotle powder, but when it's cooked with meat, the spiciness tones down. If you don't have chipotle powder, use 1 tablespoon smoked paprika plus 1 teaspoon ground chile in place of the chipotle and regular paprika.

Makes about 12 ounces

2 tablespoons butter	½ cup apple cider vinegar	½ teaspoon celery seeds
½ cup minced sweet onion (about 1 small)	¼ cup molasses	½ teaspoon kosher salt
1 cup ketchup	1 teaspoon chipotle powder	
	2 teaspoons paprika	

Melt the butter in a medium saucepan over medium heat. Add the onion and sweat it until softened and translucent, 3 to 5 minutes. Add the ketchup, vinegar, molasses, chipotle powder, paprika, celery seeds, and salt. Stir to combine. Simmer for about 20 minutes, uncovered, stirring occasionally, until thickened and darkened.

Use It For
- Brush over chicken breasts before baking or grilling.
- Mix with cooked ground beef for sloppy joes.
- Add to baked beans.
- Dipping sauce for chicken tenders.
- Mix with diced rotisserie chicken and roll in a tortilla.

Mustard-Based Barbecue Sauce

Unlike the more prevalent tomato- or vinegar-based barbecue sauces, South Carolinian barbecue has a yellowish hue from its mustard base. Settlers from Germany who arrived in the 1700s brought the spice with them. Centuries later, barbecue sauce made with mustard, vinegar, and brown sugar or molasses is readily identified as South Carolinian. You can use plain old ballpark mustard or one of this book's creamy mustards made from mustard powder rather than whole seeds. Even spicy mustard will be toned down with the cooking time of the sauce and the meat.

Makes about 14 ounces

1 cup smooth yellow mustard	¼ cup brown sugar	¼ teaspoon garlic powder
½ cup apple cider vinegar	½ teaspoon ground ginger	¼ teaspoon salt, or to taste
¼ cup molasses	¼ teaspoon ground cloves	

In a small saucepan over medium heat, whisk together the mustard, vinegar, molasses, and brown sugar until smooth. Bring to a simmer, reduce the heat to low, and simmer uncovered for 15 minutes, stirring frequently, until thickened.

Remove from the heat and stir in the ginger, cloves, garlic powder, and season with salt to taste. Transfer to a heat-safe bowl, let cool, and refrigerate, covered, for up to 1 week. The flavors of this sauce really mellow and meld in about a day, so make this sauce the day before you plan to use it.

Use It For

- Pulled Chicken: Combine 1½ pounds boneless, skinless chicken breasts and 1 chopped onion in a slow cooker. Pour the sauce over the chicken and cook for 6 hours on high or 8 to 10 hours on low. Shred the chicken before serving.
- Glaze a pork roast before cooking.
- Brush over ribs or chicken breasts before grilling.
- Toss with cubed potatoes, then roast in the oven.
- Drizzle over an open-face turkey sandwich, top with a slice of cheese, and broil.

Whiskey-Spiked Barbecue Sauce

Give your next batch of barbecued ribs a boozy kick with this barbecue sauce. I used Knob Creek Bourbon Whiskey, but any decent-quality bourbon or other whiskey will work. The alcohol cooks off, leaving just the complex, rich flavor of the spirit. If you use homemade ketchup for this recipe, you might want to add more brown sugar, as homemade ketchup isn't as sweet as commercially made ketchup.

Makes about 8 ounces

1 tablespoon butter	1 cup ketchup	½ teaspoon mustard powder
½ cup minced yellow onion (about 1 small)	2 tablespoons brown sugar	½ teaspoon ground cinnamon
	¼ cup bourbon or other whiskey	

In a medium saucepan, melt the butter over medium-low heat. Add the onion and sweat it until softened and translucent, 3 to 5 minutes. Add the ketchup, brown sugar, bourbon, mustard, and cinnamon and stir to combine. Bring to a simmer over medium heat, then reduce to low or medium-low to maintain a simmer, and cook for 20 minutes, uncovered, stirring occasionally, or until thickened.

Use It For

- Brush on pork loin before roasting.
- Slather on ribs before grilling.
- Prepare pulled chicken in the slow cooker (see page 25).
- Brush on meatloaf before cooking.
- Dipping sauce for sweet potato fries.
- Hamburger topping along with blue cheese and lettuce.

Steak Sauce

I sometimes like to eat steak solely for the pleasure of smothering it with A.1. steak sauce. There's something about the complex flavors in the sauce that is eminently satisfying. In developing my own steak sauce, I took a look at the ingredient label of A.1. to see what gives the sauce its inimitable flavor. Ingredients like raisin paste, orange, sugar, and garlic wouldn't seem to really go together, but they do so beautifully in A.1. as well as in my own sauce creation.

Makes 8 ounces

1 (6-ounce) can tomato paste	1 teaspoon grated orange zest	¼ teaspoon garlic powder
¼ cup apple cider vinegar	2 tablespoons freshly squeezed orange juice	¼ teaspoon onion powder
¼ cup white vinegar		¼ teaspoon allspice
2 teaspoons brown sugar	1 teaspoon Worcestershire sauce	¼ teaspoon mustard powder
2 tablespoons raisins	½ teaspoon salt	

In a small saucepan, heat the tomato paste over medium-low heat, stirring frequently, until it darkens slightly (a sign of caramelization, which deepens the flavor), about 3 to 5 minutes. Add the apple cider vinegar, white vinegar, brown sugar, raisins, orange zest, orange juice, Worcestershire sauce, salt, garlic powder, onion powder, allspice, and mustard powder. Stir until combined.

Simmer uncovered, over low heat stirring occasionally for 15 to 20 minutes, or until the flavors have a chance to meld. Let cool for about 5 minutes, then puree with an immersion blender or in a blender or food processor. Transfer to a sterilized jar and keep in the refrigerator for up to 1 month.

Use It For

- Condiment for steak.
- Mix into ground beef for burgers.
- Brush on pork or beef before grilling or broiling.
- Mix into meatloaf before cooking.
- Brush on portobello mushrooms before grilling.

Classic Tartar Sauce

Creamy, tangy tartar sauce can go a long way in jazzing up mild white fish like tilapia or cod. You can make homemade tartar sauce in less time than it takes the fish to cook, but it's even better if you make it a few hours before serving so that the flavors have a chance to meld.

Makes 6 ounces

½ cup mayonnaise	1 tablespoon fresh lemon juice	Dash of hot sauce or ⅛ teaspoon ground red pepper
¼ cup diced dill pickles (about 2 whole, medium pickles)	1 teaspoon Dijon or grainy mustard	Kosher salt and black pepper, to taste

In a small bowl, mix together the mayonnaise, pickles, lemon juice, mustard, and hot sauce or ground pepper. Season to taste with salt and pepper. Serve immediately or refrigerate, covered, for up to 1 day.

Variation:

Capered Tartar Sauce

Omit the mustard, substitute 2 teaspoons sweet pickle relish for the dill pickles, use only 2 teaspoons lemon juice, and add 2 tablespoons finely chopped capers and 1 tablespoon minced shallot. Use it for: condiment for smoked trout; mix with canned tuna and diced celery for tuna salad; spread on the roll or bun of a breaded fish patty sandwich; dipping sauce for fried shrimp.

Use It For

- Condiment for grilled white fish.
- Spread on a bun for a fish sandwich.
- Dipping sauce for breaded fish fillets.
- Mix with a few diced pickled jalapeños and use as a sauce for fish tacos.
- Mix with canned salmon, breadcrumbs, and an egg for salmon croquettes.

Remoulade

Originating in France, this mayonnaise-based sauce now has versions that are part of the cuisines of New Orleans, Scandinavia, and Belgium. The variations in flavors and ingredients are countless, but this is my favorite. I really love to add an anchovy to the mix, but it is entirely optional, since many people don't like the fishy flavor.

Makes 5 ounces

½ cup mayonnaise

2 teaspoons Dijon mustard

1 tablespoon chopped capers

1 tablespoon minced fresh parsley

1 tinned anchovy, minced (optional)

2 teaspoons fresh lemon juice

1 teaspoon Worcestershire sauce

½ teaspoon prepared horseradish

¼ teaspoon ground red pepper

In a small bowl, combine the mayonnaise, mustard, capers, parsley, anchovy if using, lemon juice, Worcestershire sauce, horseradish, and red pepper. Stir to combine the liquid ingredients completely. Serve immediately or refrigerate up to 2 days.

Use It For
- Condiment for cooked, chilled shrimp, lobster, or crab meat.
- Dipping sauce for french fries.
- Dollop on chilled roast beef for an appetizer or main course.
- Spread for turkey or beef sandwiches.
- Mix with boiled potatoes for potato salad.

Red Pepper Coulis

A coulis is a smooth sauce made from a fruit or vegetable that adds flavor and visual interest to a dish. With its earthy flavor and vibrant color, red pepper is a natural base for the sauce. After roasting the peppers, remove all seeds and blackened skin for a flawlessly smooth sauce.

Makes 6 to 8 ounces

1 pound red bell peppers (about 3 medium)

2 teaspoons extra virgin olive oil

1 tablespoon minced shallot (about ½ of a shallot)

¼ cup dry white wine

½ cup vegetable broth or stock

¼ teaspoon kosher salt

⅛ teaspoon black pepper

Preheat the broiler. Place the peppers on a baking sheet and set on an oven rack positioned so the peppers are 4 to 6 inches from the broiler. Turn the peppers with tongs so that all sides are evenly blackened and blistered, about 15 to 20 minutes. Place immediately in a heatproof bowl and cover tightly with plastic wrap. Let sit for 15 minutes, until cooled. Use your fingers to peel and rub the skin off. Remove the stems, seeds, and membranes. Roughly chop the peppers.

Heat the olive oil in a medium saucepan over medium-low heat. Add the shallot and sweat it until softened but not yet browned, about 3 minutes. Add the roasted pepper and sauté for 5 minutes, until softened. Stir in the white wine, increase the heat to medium, and simmer for about 5 minutes, until the liquid is nearly completely reduced.

Use It For

- Dot or drizzle on a dinner plate before plating a sliced sautéed chicken breast.
- Swirl over a bowl of cream of asparagus soup.
- Drizzle on or stir into mashed potatoes.
- Base for tomato and roasted red pepper soup.
- Chill as a dipping sauce for poached shrimp.

Add the broth and once the mixture is back to a simmer, reduce the heat to medium-low and simmer uncovered, stirring occasionally for 10 minutes or until the pepper is very soft. Let cool slightly, then puree with an immersion blender or, for a smoother sauce, transfer to a blender and puree. Season with the salt and pepper. If desired, either pass through a fine-mesh sieve or the finest disc of a food mill for a super-smooth sauce.

Prepared Horseradish Sauce

Seek out fresh horseradish root at your local supermarket or specialty grocery store and you'll be able to make your own fresh horseradish, a spicy ingredient to stir into everything from Bloody Marys to steak sauce. Look for horseradish root that appears to have been recently cut: the center should be white (rather than yellowish) and moist. It's very pungent, so I recommend using food-handling gloves to work with it.

Makes about 8 ounces

½ pound fresh horseradish root	¼ cup white vinegar, more if needed	1 teaspoon kosher salt

Use a paring knife or vegetable peeler to peel the hairy brown skin from the horseradish. Grate the root into a bowl with a fine box grater or rasp grater. Transfer the grated horseradish to the bowl of a food processor. Add about half the vinegar and half the salt and pulse to combine and further grind the horseradish. Add more vinegar until the mixture is fairly smooth and spreadable but not watery. Season to taste with additional salt. Keep covered in the refrigerator for up to 1 month (use a sterilized glass jar, as a plastic container will absorb the flavor and scent).

Use It For
- Season a Bloody Mary.
- Add a kick to tuna or chicken salad.
- Mix with mayonnaise and spread on rye bread for a roast beef sandwich.
- Stir into mashed potatoes.
- Mix with ketchup for a seafood dipping sauce.

Cocktail Sauce

As a kid, I thought the height of elegance was chilled shrimp served with tangy-spicy cocktail sauce. My mom would serve it at parties and for special occasions like New Year's Day and I always felt so sophisticated holding my shrimp by the tail and dipping it into the red sauce. While I still have a special place in my heart for the bottled brand my mom bought, I've since developed a formula for my own, highlighting the flavors I like the most (namely, the tanginess of lemon and the pungency of horseradish). This recipe has all the elements you need, and you can play around with the proportions to create a balance you like. Of course, you can use homemade ketchup (page 10) or homemade prepared horseradish (page 32) to make this sauce even more special.

Makes about 6 ounces

½ cup ketchup

1 tablespoon plus 1 teaspoon fresh lemon juice

1 tablespoon plus 1 teaspoon prepared horseradish

1 teaspoon Worcestershire sauce

1 teaspoon soy sauce

¼ teaspoon onion powder

In a small bowl, combine the ketchup, lemon juice, horseradish, Worcestershire sauce, soy sauce, and onion powder. Serve immediately or cover and refrigerate for up to 3 days.

Use It For

- Dipping sauce for poached or steamed shrimp or crab.
- Add flavor to a Bloody Mary.
- Mix into meatloaf.
- Combine with mayonnaise for a variation on Russian dressing.

Mustards & Mayonnaises

If you're used to the bland, bright-yellow ballpark mustard, be warned: homemade mustard has much more flavor and spice than commercial varieties. Heat and age can help temper the pungency though, so if you find these recipes a bit on the spicy side, letting them sit out on the counter in a covered container may help tone them down.

Mayonnaise, on the other hand, is an art in itself. The ability to make a mayonnaise from scratch is the sign of a truly accomplished cook, and it's a test that culinary students must pass. Perhaps it's because achieving a thick, creamy substance from eggs, oil, and a bit of lemon juice is the closest thing the culinary world has to true magic. But actually it's more science than magic: oil droplets are suspended in a base mixture of egg yolk, acid, water, and mustard (which helps stabilize an emulsion).

An aioli is a variation of mayonnaise from the Provence region of France. It's made with lots of garlic and uses olive oil instead of neutral vegetable oil. Both mayonnaise and aioli are versatile bases for all sorts of variations…and you'll be certain to score points with any dinner guest when you reveal that you've made your own from scratch.

Spicy Smooth Mustard

This smooth-textured mustard is spicier than the ballpark version. Adding brown sugar mellows the flavor a little; feel free to add more if you prefer a sweeter mustard.

Makes 6 ounces

½ cup mustard powder
¼ cup cold water
6 tablespoons white wine vinegar

1 teaspoon turmeric
½ teaspoon kosher salt
¼ teaspoon paprika

¼ teaspoon garlic powder
1 teaspoon brown sugar, or to taste

Place the mustard powder in a small bowl. Add the cold water all at once and use a small whisk to stir the mixture together until it forms a smooth paste. Gradually stir in the vinegar, whisking constantly to avoid lumps. Stir in the turmeric, salt, paprika, and garlic powder. Add the brown sugar to taste. Spoon into a sterilized jar and keep in the refrigerator for up to 1 month.

To make the mustard milder and less pungent, cover the bowl with plastic wrap and leave it out at room temperature instead of immediately spooning it into a jar. Taste it after 3 days, and leave it out for up to a week until it reaches the desired degree of spiciness. Then spoon into a jar.

Use It For
- Slather on hot dogs and hamburgers.
- Spread on bread before grilling a cheese sandwich.
- Stir a spoonful into a meatloaf mixture.
- Dip for a soft pretzel.
- Add a spoonful to tuna salad.

Grainy Porter Mustard

Beer and mustard have a natural affinity and porter, with its hoppy flavor and slight sweetness, is a particularly good match. If you like this recipe, try experimenting with other kinds of flavorful beers to get different results.

Makes about 6 ounces

⅛ cup yellow mustard seeds

⅛ cup brown mustard seeds

¼ cup plus 1½ teaspoons apple cider vinegar, divided

⅛ cup porter beer

2 teaspoons honey

¼ teaspoon kosher salt

In a small bowl, combine the yellow and brown mustard seeds, ¼ cup vinegar, and the beer. Cover tightly with plastic wrap, and let sit at room temperature for at least 3 days and up to a week to hydrate the seeds and allow the flavors to mellow.

Transfer the mustard mixture to a small food processor and process until mostly smooth, about 45 seconds to 1 minute. Add the remaining 1½ teaspoons vinegar along with the honey and salt and process until the mixture reaches the desired consistency. The mustard should be smooth but with some whole seeds still remaining to create texture.

Transfer to a sterilized jar. Let sit at room temperature for up to a week until the heat tones down to the desired level before refrigerating. Keep in the refrigerator for up to 1 month.

Use It For

- Burger topping along with caramelized onions and blue cheese.
- Stir a dollop into mac and cheese.
- Spread on pork chops before grilling.
- Add to potato salad.
- Mix with equal parts cream cheese, and heat gently to make a warm dip for pretzels.

Champagne-Dill Mustard

If you have champagne or sparkling wine left over from a celebration, it's the perfect time to make this mustard. The champagne gives it tartness and a light-tasting quality.

Makes about 6 ounces

⅛ cup yellow mustard seeds	¼ cup apple cider vinegar	¼ teaspoon kosher salt
⅛ cup brown mustard seeds	¼ cup champagne, divided	1 tablespoon minced fresh dill
	2 teaspoons honey	

In a small bowl, combine the yellow and brown mustard seeds, vinegar, and ⅛ cup champagne. Cover tightly with plastic wrap and let sit at room temperature for at least 3 days and up to 1 week to hydrate the seeds and allow the flavors to mellow.

Transfer the mustard mixture to a small food processor and process until mostly smooth, about 45 seconds to 1 minute. Add the remaining ⅛ cup champagne along with the honey and salt and process to combine the ingredients until they reach the desired consistency. The mustard should be smooth but with some whole seeds remaining to create texture. Stir in the dill.

Transfer to a sterilized jar. Keep the mustard in the refrigerator for up to 1 week.

Use It For
- Whisk a dollop into a cream sauce for sautéed chicken breast or pork medallions.
- Condiment for duck sausage.
- Condiment for a sandwich of smoked turkey, provolone, and sprouts.
- Stir into eggs that you're scrambling.

Honey Mustard

A classic, spicy-sweet condiment, honey mustard is a favorite, especially among kids and those with a sweet tooth. I've found that with homemade honey mustard, the flowery flavor of the honey really comes through, more so than with store-bought versions, which merely taste sweet. For this reason, use good-quality honey—you don't need a lot, and it'll really make a difference. You can experiment with different honeys; I like using local varieties with a pronounced flavor.

Makes about 6 ounces

$\frac{1}{2}$ cup mustard powder	6 tablespoons cider vinegar	$\frac{1}{4}$ teaspoon paprika
$\frac{1}{4}$ cup boiling water	1 teaspoon turmeric	$\frac{1}{8}$ teaspoon garlic powder
	$\frac{1}{2}$ teaspoon kosher salt	1 tablespoon honey

Place the mustard powder in a small bowl. Add the boiling water, using a spoon or small spatula to stir the mustard and water into a smooth paste. Stir in the vinegar. Switch to a small whisk and whisk in the turmeric, salt, paprika, and garlic powder until the mixture is smooth. Stir in the honey.

Cover the bowl with plastic wrap and let it sit at room temperature to allow the heat of the mustard to temper. Let mustard sit for up to 1 week to reach the desired level of heat, checking after the first 3 days. Transfer it to a sterilized jar and store in the refrigerator for up to 1 month.

Use It For
- Dipping sauce for chicken nuggets.
- In place of Dijon mustard in a vinaigrette.
- Spread for a sandwich with turkey, Swiss cheese, and lettuce.
- Brush on pork loin or turkey breasts before grilling or oven cooking.
- Stir a teaspoon or two into the cheese sauce for mac and cheese.

Green Chile Mustard

Green chiles give this mustard a Southwestern flavor. If you can get your hands on fresh or frozen roasted green Hatch chiles, it'll be even better! You can use the rest to make Green Chile Sauce (page 62).

Makes 6 ounces

½ cup mustard powder

4 tablespoons white wine vinegar

1 teaspoon turmeric

½ teaspoon ground cumin

½ teaspoon kosher salt

¼ teaspoon garlic powder

¼ cup hot water

3 tablespoons canned chopped green chiles

Place the mustard powder in a small bowl. Add the vinegar all at once and use a small whisk to stir the mixture together until it forms a smooth paste and is relatively free of lumps. Gradually stir in the turmeric, cumin, salt, and garlic powder until smooth. Stir in the hot water.

Cover the bowl and let it sit on the counter for several days, checking after 2 or 3 days, until the mustard reaches the desired degree of spiciness. Stir in the chiles, spoon into a sterilized jar, and keep in the refrigerator for up to 1 month.

Use It For

- Mix a spoonful into raw ground hamburger or turkey for burgers.
- Spread on pork chops before grilling.
- Mix with cream cheese and stuff into chicken breasts.
- Use in barbecue sauce recipes.

Vidalia Mustard

Sweet onions make a wonderful complement to the spicy flavor of mustard. This rustic mustard has a lot going on, both in terms of flavor and texture. Vidalia onions by definition come only from Georgia, and their level of sweetness is similar to that of a sweet apple. Find online ordering sources and information about this onion at vidaliaonion.org. Otherwise, you can find sweet onions in most well-stocked produce departments.

Makes about 8 ounces

½ cup mustard powder

¼ cup yellow mustard seeds

½ cup apple cider vinegar

½ cup hot water

1 teaspoon turmeric

½ teaspoon kosher salt

¼ teaspoon paprika

¼ teaspoon garlic powder

1 teaspoon extra virgin olive oil

½ cup minced Vidalia or other sweet onion (about 1 small)

1 tablespoon brown sugar

In a small bowl, combine the mustard powder, mustard seeds, vinegar, hot water, turmeric, salt, paprika, and garlic powder. Stir to combine until the mixture is smooth. Cover the bowl and let it sit at room temperature for up to 1 week, tasting after 3 days to see if the mixture has mellowed and reached the desired heat level. When it has, add the prepared onion.

To prepare the onion, heat the oil in a small skillet over medium heat. Add the onion and cook until translucent and slightly golden, about 5 minutes. Add the sugar and cook until syrupy, an additional 2 to 3 minutes. Remove from the heat and allow to cool to room temperature. After stirring the onion mixture into the mustard, transfer to a sterilized jar and keep in the refrigerator for up to 2 weeks.

Use It For

- Spread on roast beef sandwiches.
- Mix with mayonnaise for a burger spread.
- Whisk into a cream sauce for chicken.

Basic Mayonnaise

Mayonnaise is easy to make from scratch, and it has a creamier, more complex flavor than the store-bought version. The disadvantage is that it does not keep as long as commercially prepared mayonnaise. A batch of homemade mayo should be used within a few days, whereas many store-bought mayos will last for months in the refrigerator. If you don't think you can use up the entire amount within a few days, the recipe is easy to cut in half. (Hint: If you don't have a ½ tablespoon measuring spoon, half of 1 tablespoon is 1 ½ teaspoons.) It's best to use pasteurized eggs in this recipe (the carton will be labeled "pasteurized"), since the eggs won't be cooked and consuming raw eggs could put you at risk for salmonella.

Makes 8 to 10 ounces

2 pasteurized egg yolks

1 tablespoon white vinegar

1 tablespoon water

1 teaspoon mustard powder

1 cup vegetable or corn oil

1 teaspoon kosher salt, or more as needed

2 teaspoons fresh lemon juice, or more as needed

In a medium bowl, add the egg yolks, vinegar, water, and mustard. Whisk the ingredients until the mixture is smooth and foamy, about 1 minute.

Measure the oil in a liquid measuring cup with a spout. While whisking, slowly drizzle the oil into the egg mixture, adding only a few drops at a time and making sure that the oil is incorporated completely after each addition. The mayonnaise should become thick and creamy (though not quite as thick as commercial mayonnaise). You will need most of, but possibly not all, the oil. Stir in the salt and lemon juice, adding more to taste if needed. Use immediately or store, covered, in the refrigerator for up to 3 days.

Food Processor Method:
In the bowl of a food processor, add the egg yolks, vinegar, water, and mustard. Turn the food processor on and pulse to combine. With the motor running, slowly drizzle the oil, a few drops at a time, through the feed tube. Eventually the mixture will begin to thicken. Continue to slowly drizzle in the oil until you've achieved a thick, creamy consistency (you may not need all of the oil). Add the salt and lemon juice and pulse to combine. Stir in more salt and lemon juice to taste, if desired.

Variations:

Tarragon Mayonnaise

Increase the lemon juice to 1 tablespoon and add 3 tablespoons minced fresh tarragon when you add the salt. Use it for: elegant chicken salad with grapes and walnuts; dipping sauce for chilled poached shrimp; brush onto salmon before breading with panko crumbs and baking; mix into a creamy salad dressing.

Bacon Mayonnaise

Drizzle in 1 teaspoon cooled, liquid bacon fat just before adding the oil. When it is time to add the salt and lemon juice, add 3 strips finely chopped cooked bacon. Use it for: "Double B" BLT; toss with tomato chunks for a salad; in deviled egg filling; condiment for a club sandwich.

Dilly Horseradish Mayonnaise

Increase the lemon juice to 1 tablespoon and add 2 tablespoons prepared horseradish and 2 tablespoons chopped fresh dill (2 to 3 teaspoons if using dried) when you add the salt. Use it for: salmon cakes (add a tablespoon or two to canned salmon along with a beaten egg and some breadcrumbs, form into patties, and sauté); dipping sauce for roasted asparagus; stir into cooked salmon along with diced red onion for salmon salad or topping for toasted bagels; condiment for a roast beef and cheddar sandwich.

Dijon Mayonnaise

Substitute 1 tablespoon Dijon mustard for the mustard powder. When it is time to mix in the mustard, use 1 teaspoon and add the remaining 2 teaspoons when adding the salt and lemon juice. Use it for: egg salad with a kick; in a creamy dressing such as ranch; in a grilled ham and cheese sandwich; brush on raw fish or chicken fillets, coat in breadcrumbs, and bake.

Use It For

- Dipping sauce for french fries.
- Base for a remoulade.
- Spread on toast for a killer BLT.
- Egg salad: stir into chopped hard-cooked eggs with fresh dill or diced pickles.
- Lobster roll: toss with chopped cooked lobster and a squeeze of lemon and serve on brioche or a top-split hot dog bun.
- Slather on fish or chicken, roll in panko breadcrumbs, and bake.

Sun-Dried Tomato Mayonnaise

Sun-dried tomatoes give a slightly sweet, rich flavor to this mayonnaise. You'll be surprised by how many things it goes with!

Makes 7 ounces

½ cup sun-dried tomatoes, whole or in strips (about 2 ounces)	1 ½ teaspoons white vinegar	½ teaspoon kosher salt
	1 ½ teaspoons water	2 teaspoons fresh lemon juice
1 pasteurized egg yolk	½ teaspoon mustard powder	
	½ cup corn oil	

Bring 1 cup of water to a boil in a saucepan or the microwave. Place the sun-dried tomatoes in a small bowl and pour the boiling water over them. Let sit for 20 minutes, until the tomatoes have softened and plumped up. Drain the tomatoes, turn into a clean dish towel, and squeeze dry. Chop the tomatoes and set aside.

In a food processor, add the egg yolk, vinegar, water, and mustard. Turn the food processor on and pulse to combine. With the motor running, slowly drizzle the oil, a few drops at a time, through the feed tube. Eventually the mixture will begin to thicken. Continue to slowly drizzle in the oil until you've achieved a thick, creamy consistency (you may not need all of the oil). Add the salt and lemon juice and pulse to combine.

Add the tomatoes to the mayonnaise mixture and process just until the tomatoes are mixed into the mayonnaise and the mixture appears mostly smooth. Use immediately or store, covered, in the refrigerator, for up to 3 days.

Use It For

- Mix with canned tuna and chopped onion for tuna salad.
- Slather on raw chicken breasts, coat with panko breadcrumbs, and bake.
- Stir in ketchup and use as a dressing for a Reuben sandwich.
- Spread for a veggie wrap with avocados, sprouts, and provolone cheese.

Chipotle Lime Mayonnaise

Spicy, smoky chipotle chile peppers and lime give this mayonnaise a Southwestern vibe. To give it even more of a Tex-Mex flavor, you could stir in a teaspoon or two of ground cumin. Use canned chipotles in adobo; you'll be using one of the canned peppers as well as a little of the seasoned tomato puree in which it's packed.

Makes 7 ounces

1 pasteurized egg yolk	½ teaspoon mustard powder	½ teaspoon kosher salt
1 ½ teaspoons white vinegar	½ cup corn oil	2 teaspoons lime juice
1 ½ teaspoons water	1 canned chipotle chile pepper, minced, and 1 tablespoon adobo sauce	

In a food processor, add the egg yolk, vinegar, water, and mustard. Turn the food processor on and pulse to combine. With the motor running, slowly drizzle the oil, a few drops at a time, through the feed tube. Eventually the mixture will begin to thicken. Continue to slowly drizzle in the oil until you've achieved a thick, creamy consistency (you may not need all of the oil). Add the chipotle and adobo sauce, salt, and lime juice. Process just until the chipotle and adobo sauce are mixed into the mayonnaise and the mixture appears mostly smooth. Use immediately or store, covered, in the refrigerator, for up to 3 days.

Use It For
- Southwestern-style BLT with avocado.
- Drizzle over grilled shrimp tacos.
- Slather on toast for a fried egg sandwich.
- Brush on tilapia before baking.

Classic Aioli

If you're a fan of garlic, chances are you'll love aioli, since it's really the star in this pungent, creamy sauce—particularly since it's raw. I grate garlic cloves on a rasp grater (like a Microplane) because it gives it a finer texture than trying to chop the cloves by hand. Olive oil comes in a wide range of flavor profiles, from subtle to sharp and grassy. Because olive oil is the dominant ingredient in this recipe, I recommend a mild, subtle-tasting olive oil. You could also use a combination of olive oil and neutral-flavored grapeseed oil for an even milder result.

Makes about 6 ounces

1 pasteurized egg yolk

1 teaspoon minced garlic (about 1 medium clove)

⅛ teaspoon kosher salt, or more to taste

1 teaspoon water

½ cup extra virgin olive oil

1 tablespoon fresh lemon juice

In a medium bowl, whisk together the egg yolk, garlic, salt, and water. Gradually whisk in the olive oil, a few drops at a time, making sure the oil is incorporated completely before adding more. Continue slowly adding oil until the mixture emulsifies into a thick consistency and all the oil is integrated. Stir in the lemon juice and season to taste with additional salt, if desired.

Variations:

Basil Aioli

Combine the lemon juice with ¼ cup roughly chopped basil in a food chopper or food processor, and pulse to finely mince the basil. Set aside and add after the salt. Use it for: sandwiches of sliced tomatoes on baguette; spread for a wrap of sliced turkey breast and fresh mozzarella; dipping sauce for grilled vegetables; stir into pasta salad.

Lemony Aioli

Add 1 teaspoon finely grated lemon zest with the garlic and salt, and increase the lemon juice to 2 tablespoons. Use it for: toss with diced cooked

Use It For
- Dipping sauce for crisp-tender steamed vegetables, such as new potatoes, asparagus, or green beans.
- Drizzle over poached salmon.
- Add to potato salad with chives and minced roasted red peppers.
- Condiment for lamb burgers.

potatoes for potato salad; dip for steamed artichoke leaves; drizzle on crab cakes; condiment for lobster rolls.

Roasted Red Pepper Aioli

Preheat the broiler. Place 1 medium red bell pepper on a baking sheet and set on an oven rack positioned so the pepper is 4 to 6 inches from the broiler. Turn with tongs so all sides of the pepper are evenly blackened and blistered, about 15 to 20 minutes. Place immediately in a heatproof bowl and cover tightly with plastic wrap. Let sit for 15 minutes, until cooled. Use your fingers to peel and rub the skin off. Remove the stem, seeds, and membranes. Roughly chop the pepper, transfer to a small food processor, and puree—or place in a small bowl and puree with an immersion blender. Prepare the aioli according to directions, eliminating the lemon juice. Gently fold in the pepper puree. Use it for: topping for a grilled fish sandwich; dip for crudité or sweet potato fries; mix into chicken salad with chopped celery, halved grapes, and sliced almond; drizzle over grilled asparagus.

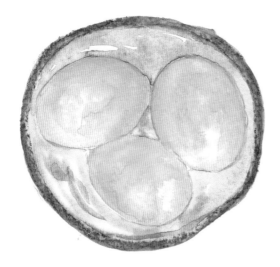

Pickles & Relishes

Pickled vegetables and fruits have been around for thousands of years in one form or another. In his book *On Food and Cooking*, Harold McGee defines pickles as "a food preserved by immersion in brine or a strong acid such as vinegar." The brine—a salt and liquid solution—encourages fermentation, which acts as a preservative, while vinegar inhibits the growth of microbes.

The pickle and relish recipes in this book are of the vinegar-preserved variety, and most can be enjoyed immediately or canned to enjoy a few months from now. If you're canning these pickles and relishes, be sure to read the appendix on Food Safety and Canning (page 116).

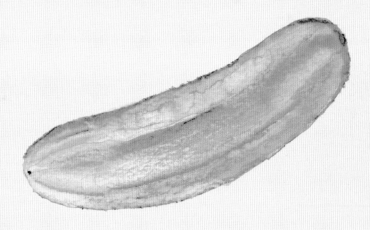

Dill Pickles

There's nothing like a crisp, puckery-sour dill pickle. Commercial products often contain high fructose corn syrup, so I'm glad making pickles from scratch is easy. Pickling spice is sold with canning equipment, in supermarkets, or at spice companies like Penzey's. It usually consists of a complex mixture of such spices as mustard seeds, peppercorns, allspice, peppers, and coriander.

Makes 3 pints

2 pounds pickling cucumbers	3 tablespoons granulated sugar	3 medium cloves garlic, quartered
3 cups water	3 tablespoons pickling spice	
3 cups white vinegar	3 tablespoons chopped fresh dill or 1 tablespoon dry dill	$\frac{3}{8}$ teaspoon pickle crisp (optional)
$\frac{1}{3}$ cup canning salt		

Wash the cucumbers, trim the stems, and cut into long spears, trimming if needed so they'll fit vertically in jars with about $\frac{1}{4}$ inch headspace. (Or slice them into chips to fit more into a jar.) Sterilize jars and let sit in hot water to keep jars hot until needed (see canning and sterilizing instructions on page 118).

In a medium saucepan, combine the water, vinegar, salt, sugar, and pickling spice. Bring to a simmer over medium-high heat, then reduce the heat to medium-low and simmer for about 15 minutes to infuse the flavor. Strain into a bowl (discard the pickling spice) and stir in the dill.

Working with one hot pint jar at a time, pack in the pickles, adding a couple pieces of garlic to each jar. Sprinkle with Pickle Crisp (see note below), if using. Ladle in the pickling liquid, leaving $\frac{1}{4}$ inch headspace. Adjust the lids, place in a boiling water canner, and process for 10 minutes. Let cool completely.

Note: You can find pickle crisp, a type of salt that acts as a firming agent, in your supermarket's canning department. Don't confuse it with canning salt, which won't give you the same result. To use it, sprinkle about $\frac{1}{8}$ teaspoon into each jar over the pickles before you top off with the liquid.

Use It For
- On hot dogs and hamburgers.
- Dice and add to mayonnaise for tartar sauce.
- Dice and stir into tuna salad.
- On a submarine sandwich.

Bread and Butter Pickles

Whenever I make bread and butter pickles I am fondly reminded of my old friend Marty, who excels at everything he does. After graduating from culinary school, he invited me to his Tribeca apartment for a delicious lunch and sent me home with a jar of bread and butter pickles he'd canned. I went back to my apartment and opened the jar. The pickles were so tasty that before I knew it, I'd eaten the whole jar.

Makes 3 pints

3 pounds pickling cucumbers, sliced ¼ inch thick

2 medium yellow onions, halved and thinly sliced

¼ cup canning salt

2 cups granulated sugar

2 cups white vinegar

1 tablespoon yellow mustard seeds

1 teaspoon celery seeds

1 teaspoon ground ginger

1 teaspoon whole peppercorns, black or pink

½ teaspoon whole cloves

1 teaspoon turmeric

⅜ teaspoon Pickle Crisp, see page 50 (optional)

In a large bowl, combine the cucumber and onion slices. Sprinkle the salt over the top and stir to combine. Cover with a layer of ice and refrigerate for about 3 hours to allow time for the salt to draw out excess moisture. Drain and rinse. Sterilize jars and let sit in hot water to keep jars hot until needed (see canning and sterilizing instructions on page 118).

In a large saucepan, combine the sugar, vinegar, mustard seeds, celery seeds, ginger, peppercorns, cloves, and turmeric. Bring to a simmer over medium heat, then reduce the heat to low and simmer for about 10 minutes to allow the flavors to meld.

Add the cucumber and onion, and reheat to boiling over medium heat. Fill hot pint jars with the pickles, cooking liquid, and Pickle Crisp (see previous page), if using, leaving ¼-inch headspace. Adjust the lids, place in a boiling water canner, and process for 10 minutes. Let cool completely.

Use It For

- Topping for hamburgers.
- Dice and add to tuna or chicken salad.
- Dice and use as hot dog relish.
- Condiment with pulled pork.
- Mix into potato salad.

Asian Quick Pickles

This light and refreshing preparation is quick and easy to whip up at a moment's notice. Rice vinegar isn't acidic enough for safe canning (it has a little more than 4 percent, whereas canning requires vinegar with an acidity of at least 5 percent), so these pickles are best eaten immediately or stored in the refrigerator for up to 3 days.

Makes about 12 ounces

¾ cup unseasoned rice vinegar

1 tablespoon granulated sugar

¼ teaspoon kosher salt or sea salt

1 medium daikon radish

2 medium carrots

1 medium English cucumber

2 tablespoons chopped fresh cilantro

1 green onion (white part), thinly sliced

1 tablespoon sesame seeds

In a small saucepan, combine the vinegar, sugar, and salt and bring to a boil over medium heat. Remove from the heat and let the sugar and salt dissolve completely.

Peel the daikon, carrots, and cucumber. Using a knife or a mandoline, thinly slice the daikon and carrots on the diagonal. Then stack a few slices at a time and cut into matchsticks. Halve the cucumber lengthwise, scoop out the seeds with a spoon, and thinly slice into crescents.

Place all the vegetables in a medium bowl and pour the vinegar mixture over the top. Add the cilantro and green onion and toss to combine. Sprinkle with the sesame seeds.

Use It For
- Topping for a bowl of ramen noodles.
- Condiment for a Vietnamese banh mi sandwich.
- Topping for chilled sesame noodles.
- Filling for spring rolls along with seasoned, cooked ground pork.
- Condiment for grilled salmon or tuna.

Corn and Pepper Relish

This fresh-tasting relish is fantastic in the summertime when you can use in-season corn and red peppers. But if fresh corn isn't available, you can use thawed frozen kernels. This relish is bulky enough to serve as a side salad, but it also works beautifully as a condiment on so many things.

Makes 1½ pints

2 cups cooked corn kernels (from about 3 ears of corn)

2 cups diced red bell pepper (about 2 large peppers)

½ cup diced red onion (about 1 small)

2 cups white vinegar

1 cup water

¼ cup granulated sugar

2 teaspoons dill seeds

1 teaspoon celery seeds

½ teaspoon mustard powder

1 teaspoon kosher salt

½ teaspoon turmeric

Sterilize jars and let sit in hot water to keep jars hot until needed (see canning and sterilizing instructions on page 118). In a large saucepan, combine the corn, bell pepper, onion, vinegar, water, sugar, dill seeds, celery seeds, mustard powder, salt, and turmeric. Bring to a simmer over medium-high heat. Reduce the heat to medium-low or low to maintain a simmer and cook for about 20 minutes. Transfer to hot pint jars. If canning, leave about ¼ inch headspace and process in a boiling water canner for 15 minutes. Otherwise, refrigerate for up to 1 month.

Use It For
- On turkey burgers.
- Mix with diced avocado for a side salad.
- Stir into chicken noodle soup.
- Topping for black bean soup.
- Condiment for grilled chicken.

Dill Relish

A hot dog is so much better when it's topped with a mound of relish. And a jar of this concoction in the fridge will come in handy for plenty of other uses as well.

Makes about 3 pints

3 pounds pickling cucumbers	3 cups apple cider vinegar	2 teaspoons mustard seeds
1 cup chopped red bell pepper, seeds and membranes removed (about ¾ pound)	2 tablespoons granulated sugar	3 medium cloves garlic, minced
	2 tablespoons canning salt	
	1 tablespoon dill seeds	

Trim the ends of the cucumbers and either finely dice them by hand or cut them into chunks and pulse in the food processor until finely chopped. Transfer to a large bowl; add the bell pepper and set aside.

Sterilize jars and let sit in hot water to keep jars hot until needed (see canning and sterilizing instructions on page 118). In a large saucepan, combine the vinegar, sugar, salt, dill seeds, mustard seeds, and garlic over medium-high heat. Bring to a boil, then reduce the heat to low and simmer for 5 minutes to dissolve the sugar and salt and allow the flavors to develop. Add the vegetables, return to a boil over medium-high heat, and simmer for 10 minutes.

Fill hot pint jars with the relish, leaving about ¼ inch headspace. Adjust the lids, place in a boiling water canner, and process for 20 minutes. Allow to cool completely.

Use It For
- Topping for hot dogs and hamburgers.
- In tartar sauce.
- Stir into tuna or egg salad.
- In deviled egg filling.
- Add to sloppy joe mixture.

Sweet Pickle Relish

This sweet-and-tart version of pickle relish is very much like the kind you'll find at the ballpark, minus the high fructose corn syrup and artificial additives.

Makes about 3 pints

3 pounds pickling cucumbers	1 medium yellow onion, minced	1 tablespoon mustard seeds
1 cup chopped red bell pepper, seeds and membranes removed (about 2 medium peppers)	¼ cup canning salt	1 teaspoon celery seeds
	1 cup granulated sugar	1 teaspoon ground ginger
	3 cups cider vinegar	1 teaspoon turmeric
		1 teaspoon whole cloves

Trim the ends of the cucumbers and either finely dice them by hand or cut them into chunks and pulse in the food processor until finely chopped. Transfer to a large bowl; add the bell pepper and onion. Sprinkle with salt and add enough water and ice to cover the vegetables. Cover with plastic wrap and let stand for 2 hours. Drain, rinse in a colander, and drain completely.

In a large saucepan, combine the sugar, vinegar, mustard seeds, celery seeds, ginger, turmeric, and cloves. Bring to a simmer over medium-high heat, then reduce the heat to low and simmer for 10 minutes to allow the flavors to meld. Strain out whole spices, then return the liquid to the pan. Add the vegetables, heat to a simmer over medium heat, and reduce heat to low to simmer for 10 minutes, allowing flavors to develop.

Ladle the relish and liquid into hot pint jars, leaving ¼ inch headspace. Adjust the lids, place in a boiling water canner, and process for 15 minutes. Let cool completely.

Use It For
- On hot dogs or sausages.
- Stir into egg salad.
- Topping for a fried egg sandwich.
- Sandwich filling along with finely diced cooked ham and mayonnaise.

Hot Sauces & Salsas

A dash of hot sauce can liven up anything from a scrambled egg to a bowl of soup. And salsas are great for far more than simply a dip for chips: salsa is as ubiquitous in Latin cuisine as ketchup is in the U.S. It's fun to make your own of both so you can control heat levels, experiment with different types of chile peppers, and add favorite seasonings. The trick is to find a good source for a wide variety of chiles. If your supermarket's produce section is limited to only the basics, try international, Asian, or Hispanic grocery stores; farmer's markets; or even online sources. And take care when handling the peppers. When you touch chile peppers, even if you wash your hands well afterward, the oils can linger on your skin and cause irritation when you rub your eyes, nose, or other sensitive body parts. I like to keep a box of disposable gloves on hand for working with peppers.

Tangy Two-Pepper Sauce

Use a super-spicy red habanero pepper, along with a milder pepper, to customize this fresh, tangy sauce to your preferred heat level. Red bell peppers, piquillo peppers, and cubanelles are all good choices for flavorful but heat-free peppers to make up the bulk of this sauce. How to know if a pepper is going to be spicy or mild? Typically, the tinier the pepper, the more heat it packs. What's more, the heat is concentrated in the seeds and white membranes, so clean these away from the flesh of the pepper to better control the spice.

Makes 6 to 8 ounces

8 ounces mild red chile or sweet peppers, such as bell pepper or cubanelle, seeded and diced

1 teaspoon diced habanero chile pepper, seeds and membranes removed, or more to taste

2 medium cloves garlic, roughly chopped

1 teaspoon kosher salt

½ cup white vinegar

1 ½ teaspoons granulated sugar

¼ teaspoon garlic powder (optional)

Place the mild and habanero peppers, garlic, salt, vinegar, and sugar in a small saucepan over medium heat. Bring to a simmer, reduce the heat to low, cover, and cook for 20 minutes, or until the peppers have softened. Note: Be sure that when you lift the lid, you hold it so that the steam rises away from your face—inhaling spicy vapors can be painful!

Remove from the heat, uncover, and let cool for 15 minutes. Transfer the pepper mixture to a blender and process at medium speed for 45 seconds to 1 minutes, scraping down the sides as needed, until the mixture is mostly smooth. Season to taste with more salt and with garlic powder if using. Let cool, then transfer to a sterilized jar. The sauce will last in the refrigerator for up to 1 month.

Use It For
- Shake over scrambled eggs wrapped in flour tortillas.
- Add a kick to egg salad or tuna salad.
- Topping for french fries or roasted potatoes.
- Stir into black bean soup.

Rooster-Style Sauce

Sriracha sauce is a favorite Asian condiment, originating in Thailand. But it was popularized here in the U.S. when a Vietnamese immigrant founded Huy Fong Foods in Los Angeles in 1980 and started producing a version. Fans of the sauce have found that it's fantastic on just about everything, and my version of this iconic sauce is similarly versatile. Fresno chiles or red jalapeños, which have a medium heat, are the best to use in this sauce, but you can also experiment with other red chiles in the medium-hot range (or mix a small amount of a very hot chile with a larger quantity of a milder one).

Makes about 8 ounces

8 ounces red jalapeño chile peppers, seeds and membranes removed, chopped

½ cup apple cider vinegar

2 tablespoons brown sugar

2 medium cloves garlic

1 teaspoon kosher salt

In a medium saucepan over medium heat, combine the jalapeño, vinegar, brown sugar, garlic, and salt. Bring to a simmer, then reduce the heat to low and simmer for 20 minutes or until the jalapeño has softened.

Let the mixture cool for about 15 minutes, then transfer to a blender and blend until smooth. Pour into a sterilized jar and keep refrigerated for up to 1 month.

Use It For

- Pizza topping.
- Stir into Asian noodle soups.
- Sprinkle on stir-fry.
- Stir into hollandaise sauce for poached eggs.
- Mix into mashed avocado with lime juice and salt, and spread on crackers.

Key Lime–Jalapeño Sauce

Perhaps with my love for Key lime pie in mind, my mother-in-law brought me back a souvenir from her trip to the Florida Keys: a bottle of Key lime hot sauce. The combination of tart and spicy was addictive and for a while I was dousing everything with it, until I ran out. Until she goes back to the Keys (or, better yet, I plan a trip there myself), I have been re-creating that sauce as best I can when I am able to find bags of Key limes at a specialty produce store. I've seen bottled Key lime juice if you can't find the fresh fruit.

Makes 5 ounces

¼ cup Key lime juice, preferably fresh (about 6 limes)

⅔ cup chopped jalapeño chile peppers, seeds and membranes removed (about 2 large)

½ teaspoon kosher salt

2 tablespoons white vinegar

¼ teaspoon ground cumin

¼ teaspoon garlic powder

Combine the lime juice, jalapeño, salt, vinegar, cumin, and garlic powder in a blender. Process until the jalapeño is finely chopped and the ingredients are well mixed. (Alternatively, you can put the ingredients in a bowl and mix them with an immersion blender.)

Transfer the ingredients to a sterilized jar and store in the refrigerator for up to 1 month. The hot sauce will be a little chunky, so be sure to stir or shake it before using.

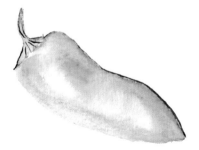

Use It For
- Stir into a Bloody Mary.
- Topping for scrambled eggs.
- Add a dash to tuna salad or potato salad.
- Spice up burritos and tacos.
- Add spice and flavor to salsa or pico de gallo.

Mom's Red Chile Sauce

My mother lives in New Mexico, where she grew up eating just about everything from eggs to enchiladas smothered in thick, spicy red chile sauce. It was also a Friday night mainstay when I was growing up. When I first started cooking, I asked Mom to show me how she made it. On the first attempt, she was so used to doing it by rote that she couldn't really convey the measurements and the technique. We did finally master it, and now I am making red chile sauce for my own family, with ground chiles that Mom sends me from Santa Fe. It's important to use ground red chiles (interchangeably called chile powder) for this recipe—they're usually called Hatch red chiles, named for the region in which they're grown. One online source is Los Chileros (www.loschileros.com).

Makes about 16 ounces

1 tablespoon vegetable oil	½ cup ground chile powder	½ teaspoon kosher salt
1 tablespoon all-purpose flour	2 cups hot water	1 tablespoon tomato paste
	½ teaspoon garlic powder	

In a medium skillet, heat the oil over medium heat. Add the flour and whisk or stir with a wooden spoon until the flour is clumpy and pasty, about 1 minute. Add the ground chile powder and cook, whisking constantly for an additional minute to toast the chile.

Pour in the hot water while stirring and whisk until the mixture is smooth and free of lumps. Stir in the garlic powder, salt, and tomato paste. Bring to a simmer over medium heat, then reduce the heat to low and cook, stirring frequently for 10 to 15 minutes until the sauce has thickened. Serve immediately or refrigerate, covered, for up to 3 days.

Use It For

- Spoon over burritos, sprinkle with cheese, and broil.
- On huevos rancheros, or drizzle over fried or scrambled eggs.
- Topping for enchiladas.
- Dipping sauce for fresh flour tortillas.

Green Chile Sauce

Like the red chile sauce in the previous recipe, green chile sauce is a mainstay of New Mexican cuisine. At restaurants, the wait staff will ask you "Red, green, or Christmas?" As you might guess, the last option means both red and green. For this recipe you will need roasted or canned green chiles. Roasted chiles, if you can get your hands on them, are better as I've found that the canned versions don't have much heat. Some New Mexican chile farmers will ship roasted green chiles frozen. One to try: New Mexican Connection (newmexicanconnection.com). If you must use canned, and you find that the heat isn't intense enough, try adding some diced jalapeños to the sauce.

Makes about 12 ounces

1 tablespoon vegetable oil	½ teaspoon garlic powder	1 cup chopped roasted green chiles
¼ cup diced yellow onion	½ teaspoon ground cumin	
1 tablespoon all-purpose flour	1 teaspoon dried Mexican oregano or Italian oregano	½ cup water
		½ teaspoon kosher salt

In a medium saucepan, heat the oil over medium heat. Add the onion and sweat it, stirring frequently, until softened, 3 to 5 minutes. Sprinkle the flour, garlic powder, cumin, and oregano over the onion and cook, stirring, until the mixture forms dry clumps, about 1 minute.

Add the chiles, water, and salt and stir to combine. Simmer, uncovered and stirring occasionally, for about 20 minutes or until the sauce has thickened. Use as is or puree for a smoother texture. Use immediately or refrigerate, covered, for up to 3 days.

Use It For
- Sauce for enchiladas.
- On grilled fish or chicken tacos.
- Stir into eggs that you're scrambling.
- Mix with sour cream to make a dip for tortilla chips.

Black Bean and Corn Salsa

This hearty salsa comes together in minutes with mostly canned and frozen ingredients. It's almost thick enough to serve as a salad and is a wonderful topping for many Southwestern and Mexican dishes.

Makes about 24 ounces

1 (15½-ounce) can black beans, drained and rinsed (or about 1¾ cups cooked black beans)

1½ cups cooked fresh or frozen and thawed yellow corn kernels

6 to 7 ounces tomatoes, seeded and diced (about 2 medium slicing tomatoes)

¼ cup minced red onion

2 teaspoons minced jalapeño chile pepper, seeds and membranes removed, or to taste

2 tablespoons minced fresh cilantro

2 tablespoons fresh lime juice (about 1 lime)

½ teaspoon salt, or to taste

In a large bowl, combine the beans, corn, tomato, onion, jalapeño, and cilantro, stirring gently with a spoon to mix. Drizzle the lime juice over the mixture, sprinkle with salt, stir to combine, and adjust salt, jalapeño, and lime juice as needed. Serve immediately or refrigerate, covered, for up to 2 days.

Use It For
- Topping for grilled fish or chicken tacos.
- Spoon into scoop-style tortilla chips for an appetizer.
- In quesadillas.
- Sprinkle on huevos rancheros.
- Fold into tortillas.

Pico de Gallo

This fresh, tangy salsa is a staple in Mexican and Southwestern cuisines. Spanish for "rooster's beak," pico de gallo was supposedly named for the way it was eaten at one time, pinched between the thumb and finger, like a pecking beak, according to Sharon Tyler Herbst in The Food Lover's Companion. *It mixes up quickly in a food processor, but if you prefer a chunkier version, you can finely chop the ingredients by hand.*

Makes 10 to 12 ounces

10 ounces tomatoes (about 3 medium slicer tomatoes), seeded and quartered

½ cup chopped red onion (about ¾ of a small onion)

½ cup roughly chopped fresh cilantro

2 teaspoons minced jalapeño chile pepper, seeds and membranes removed, or to taste

1 tablespoon lime juice (about ½ lime)

1 teaspoon kosher salt

Combine the tomatoes, onion, cilantro, jalapeño, lime juice, and salt in a food processor and pulse a few times until chopped and combined, but still chunky. Store the sauce, tightly covered, in the refrigerator for up to 2 days.

Use It For
- Topping for burritos and tacos.
- Dip for tortilla chips.
- Topping or dipping sauce for grilled fish or chicken.
- Marinade for steak before grilling.
- Topping for a taco salad.

Avocado-Tomatillo Salsa

This is one of my favorite salsas: a medley of contrasts in flavor and texture, even if it's pretty much all shades of the same color. Plus it's a great showcase for tomatillos, which have a tangy flavor that is a delicious foil for the creamy avocado. Most supermarkets carry fresh tomatillos in their produce sections these days, but if you can't find them at your local store, check out a natural foods store or a Mexican produce stand. For visual contrast, try adding diced red bell pepper.

Makes about 20 ounces

1 pound tomatillos, papery husks removed, rinsed and diced

2 medium avocados, diced

1 tablespoon minced green onion, white part

2 tablespoons minced cilantro (optional)

1 teaspoon minced red habanero or red jalapeño chile pepper (optional)

1 tablespoon lime juice (about ½ lime)

Kosher salt to taste

In a bowl, combine the tomatillo, avocado, green onion, cilantro, and chile pepper if using. Gently stir with a spoon to mix well without mashing the avocado pieces.

Sprinkle the lime juice and salt over top and stir to combine. Serve immediately as the avocado will turn brown after a few hours, although tossing it in extra lime juice will help prolong its freshness. (Browned avocado can still be eaten—it's just a matter of aesthetics.)

Use It For

- On its own, folded into a warm corn tortilla for a taco.
- Topping for grilled tuna.
- Atop brown rice.
- Turkey burger topping along with queso fresco and sprouts.

Tropical Salsa

Fresh tropical fruits make a beautiful spicy-sweet salsa that is perfect for summertime meals. While this recipe calls for mango and pineapple, you can substitute other complementary fruits, such as papaya, kiwi, grapefruit, and guava.

Makes about 10 ounces

1 ½ cups diced mango (about 2 medium)

2 cups chopped fresh pineapple

¼ cup loosely packed chopped fresh cilantro

1 tablespoon minced red onion

1 teaspoon minced jalapeño chile pepper, seeds and membranes removed

2 tablespoons fresh lemon or lime juice

¼ teaspoon kosher salt

In a large bowl, combine the mango, pineapple, cilantro, red onion, and jalapeño. Sprinkle the citrus juice and salt over top and toss to combine. The salsa will keep, tightly covered, in the refrigerator for up to 2 days.

Use It For
- Relish for grilled fish or shrimp.
- Dip for tortilla chips.
- Topping for grilled chicken tacos.
- Mix with diced cooked crab or lobster and spoon inside avocado halves.

Cutting a Mango

While gadgets exist for splitting and peeling mangoes, they're not necessary. All you need is a small knife (a utility or paring knife with a 4-inch blade is ideal). The important thing to know is that the mango's pit is large but fairly flat, like a giant watermelon seed. Hold the mango, stem side up, on your cutting board and cut the mango lengthwise as if you're cutting it in half, but making your cut just to one side of the middle. If you encounter the pit, simply tilt your knife blade slightly so you cut around it. Cut the other side of the mango lengthwise as well, to the other side of the stem so that you have a middle slice containing the pit, which is about $\frac{3}{4}$ inches wide, and two "halves."

To dice the mango, make cuts lengthwise and crosswise into the cut side of each mango half, cutting almost to, but not through, the skin. Bend the mango half so the exterior of the skin is concave, and cut or pull the mango chunks off the skin using a knife or your fingers. If you want to maximize the yield of your mango, you can also cut around the edge of the slice containing the pit, peeling the skin away from the edible part of the mango.

Cutting a Pineapple

To turn a fresh pineapple into a bowl full of neat chunks, you'll need a chef's knife, a large cutting board, and a small round biscuit or cookie cutter, about 1 to $1\frac{1}{2}$ inches in diameter. Begin by slicing off and discarding the top and the base of the pineapple. Standing the pineapple upright on the cutting board, make long slices of the rind from top to bottom, angling the knife to follow the slight curve of the pineapple. Continue to slice away the rind until it's completely removed. Turn the pineapple on its side and cut it into rounds of the desired thickness. Working with one slice at a time, use the biscuit cutter to punch out and discard the tough circle-shaped core at the center of each piece, so that doughnut-shaped rings remain. Cut the rings into the desired size pieces.

Or, once you've cut away the rind, you can cut the pineapple in half lengthwise and then again into several long spears. Cutting at an angle, remove the core from each spear, then slice the spears into the desired size pieces.

Infused Oils & Vinegars

Oil or vinegar flavored with an herb, fruit, or other fragrant ingredient morphs into something quite wonderful and versatile. The simple infusions on the following pages are so versatile: they can be drizzled on cooked vegetables or meats, used as a dip for hunks of bread, drizzled on salads, or used in vinaigrettes, pestos, and sauces.

Vinegar's high acidity makes it naturally antibacterial, so an infused vinegar will keep for quite some time: 2 to 3 months in a cool, dark place, or twice as long as that in the refrigerator (my recommendation). Oil, however, can be a breeding ground for bacteria, and food preserved in oil has been blamed for cases of botulism. For this reason, it's best to make only as much infused or flavored oil as you need and to use it quickly. I recommend refrigerating the infused oil and using it up within 3 days. You'll notice that the infused oil recipes in this chapter have small yields, though feel free to scale the recipe up if you need more. If you give any of these oils or vinegars as a gift, be sure to tell the recipient how to store and safely use it.

Roasted Garlic Olive Oil

This easy recipe calls for poaching cloves of garlic in olive oil in the oven, which infuses the oil with the heady, mellow flavor of the garlic. Don't throw away those poached cloves of garlic afterward. Mash them up, mix in a generous pinch of sea salt, and use as a spread for bread, as a flavoring in tomato sauce or tomato soup, or rubbed on a chicken before roasting.

Makes 4 ounces

½ cup extra virgin olive oil

5 large cloves garlic, peeled and sliced in half lengthwise

Preheat the oven to 350°F. Place the oil and garlic pieces in a small ramekin. Cover the ramekin with aluminum foil and cook in the oven for about 30 to 45 minutes, until the garlic is soft when pierced with a fork. Remove the garlic (save to use in another application). Transfer the oil to a sterilized glass bottle or jar, and refrigerate for up to 3 days.

Use It For
- Make garlic bread.
- Drizzle over asparagus and top with shaved Parmesan cheese.
- In balsamic vinaigrette.
- Rub on chicken before roasting.
- Brush on cod before grilling.

Rosemary-Infused Oil

Rosemary is an excellent herb for making infusions, as it has a distinctive, strong flavor. I particularly like making this in the autumn and winter, because to me it has a very wintry flavor. Be sure to choose rosemary that has fresh, green leaves, and avoid stalks that look brown and dried-up.

Makes 4 ounces

½ cup extra virgin olive oil	1 sprig fresh rosemary, about 4 inches

Wash the rosemary and dry it very well by wrapping it in a few layers of paper towel or letting it air-dry for several hours on a paper towel or a clean dish towel.

Bruise the rosemary by rolling it a few times with a rolling pin, or simply squeezing and rubbing it between your fingers.

Place the oil in a small saucepan over low heat and add the rosemary sprig. Heat the oil until it is just about to simmer (it should reach about 200°F). Turn off the heat and let the rosemary sit in the pan for 20 minutes, then remove the sprig. Pour the oil into a sterilized glass bottle or jar and refrigerate for up to 3 days.

Use It For

- Brush on chicken breasts or thighs before grilling or baking.
- Dip for baguettes.
- Drizzle over steamed green beans or sautéed spinach.
- Make salad dressing.
- Sprinkle on popcorn (try an olive oil mister to get even, light coverage).

Lemon-Infused Oil

Lemon rind gives this oil a bright, citrusy flavor that makes it ideal for drizzling on fish or using as the base for a salad dressing.

Makes 4 ounces

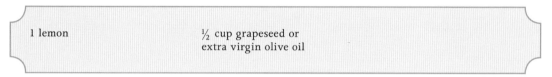

1 lemon	½ cup grapeseed or extra virgin olive oil

To prepare the lemon rind, use a paring knife to cut the ends off the lemon. Discard them. Cut the rind away from the lemon in strips, working end to end the length of the lemon, cutting away both the zest and the white part.

Place the oil and the lemon rind in a small saucepan and heat the mixture over medium-low heat. When the oil is just about to simmer (about 200°F), remove the pan from the heat and let the lemon infuse in the oil, 20 minutes to 1 hour. Use a slotted spoon to remove and discard the rind. Pour the oil into a sterilized glass bottle or jar and refrigerate for up to 3 days.

Use It For
- Dip for artichoke leaves.
- Sauté baby spinach leaves in the oil.
- Drizzle over grilled salmon.
- Make salad dressing.
- In pound cake recipes calling for oil.

Fig-Infused Vinegar

For this infusion I use black mission figs, which turn the vinegar a beautiful dark amber. The resulting vinegar is wonderfully tangy-sweet, almost like sherry vinegar or good balsamic vinegar. You'll need a little more vinegar than in the other flavored vinegar recipes since the dried figs absorb a lot of it while they're steeping.

Makes about 6 ounces

1 ½ cups white wine vinegar   1 cup quartered dried figs

Combine the vinegar and figs in a small saucepan and bring to a simmer over medium-low heat. Reduce the heat to low and let simmer, covered, for 10 minutes. Remove from the heat and let sit, covered, 1 to 3 hours to continue infusing the vinegar with the fig flavor. Strain through cheesecloth or a fine sieve into a sterilized glass bottle or jar. Keep in a dark, cool place for up to 3 months or refrigerate for up to 6 months.

Use It For

- Braise pearl onions.
- Make dressing for a spinach, dried cranberry, and goat cheese salad.
- Drizzle over fresh strawberries.
- Marinate pork chops.

Raspberry Vinegar

The fruity, fresh flavor of raspberries goes beautifully with white wine vinegar, and the raspberries make a lovely ruby-colored liquid. Be sure to use the ripest, freshest berries you can find—in this case, berries that are almost overripe (as long as they're not moldy) are better than those that are underripe.

Makes 8 ounces

1 cup fresh raspberries	1 cup white wine vinegar

Place the raspberries in a small saucepan and lightly crush them with a wooden spoon. Pour in the vinegar, stir to combine, and bring to a simmer over medium-low heat. Reduce the heat to low and let simmer, covered, for 10 minutes. Remove from the heat and let sit, covered, for 1 to 3 hours to continue infusing the vinegar with the raspberry flavor. Strain through cheesecloth or a fine sieve into a sterilized glass bottle or jar. Keep in a dark, cool place for up to 3 months or refrigerate for up to 6 months.

Use It For
- Drizzle on fruit salad.
- Add a splash to sparkling water on ice for a refreshing drink.
- Dress spinach greens and top with seared scallops.
- Mix into chicken salad.

Herbed Balsamic Vinegar

You don't need a super expensive aged balsamic for this recipe. In fact, the cooking process will concentrate the balsamic flavor a little and the herbs will enhance it, so this recipe will actually improve an inexpensive brand.

Makes 8 ounces

7 to 10 sprigs fresh thyme	1 cup balsamic vinegar

Wash the thyme and dry it by wrapping it in a few layers of paper towel or letting it air-dry for several hours on a paper towel or clean dish towel.

In a small saucepan, combine the vinegar and thyme. Bring to a simmer over medium heat. Reduce the heat to low to maintain simmer and simmer, covered, for 10 minutes to allow the flavor to infuse. Remove from the heat and let sit, covered, 1 to 3 hours to continue infusing the vinegar with the thyme flavor. Strain through cheesecloth or a fine sieve into a sterilized glass bottle or jar. Keep in a dark, cool place for up to 3 months or refrigerate for up to 6 months.

Use It For
- Toss with quartered new potatoes before roasting.
- Brush on asparagus before grilling.
- Drizzle over sliced tomatoes, fresh mozzarella, and basil.
- Reduce by simmering until syrupy and drizzle over grilled chicken.

Salad Dressings

I really don't understand why there's such a market for bottled salad dressings when homemade dressings are so incredibly quick and easy to make and the simplest ones use ingredients that you most likely have in your pantry. Most bottled dressings are chock-full of artificial flavors, preservatives, fillers, and other unhealthy ingredients.

I hope that this chapter will help demystify salad dressings and that you'll clean out your fridge door of all those bottles and instead make a fresh, quick dressing every time salad is on your menu. A word about proportions: my culinary school instructors will probably be aghast that I don't follow the classic vinaigrette proportions in my recipes. The proper proportion, as any chef will tell you, is 3 parts oil to 1 part vinegar. My personal feeling is that this formula yields a very heavy, oily vinaigrette. While I've included a recipe for a classic vinaigrette, you'll find that the rest of my recipes tend to up the proportion of non-oil ingredients, resulting in a tangy, bright-tasting dressing.

The technique for a vinaigrette is very simple: just mix the acidic ingredient (vinegar, citrus juice) with the salt (which won't dissolve as easily once the oil is added), mustard, and other flavorings, and then drizzle in the oil gradually while whisking. The whisking motion emulsifies the mixture, that is, suspends the droplets of oil in the acid so that the finished dressing is creamy and thick.

Classic Vinaigrette

As I said in the introduction to this chapter, traditional vinaigrette has a proportion of 3 parts oil to 1 part vinegar. Remember this formula and you'll be able to make an endless variety of vinaigrettes with different types of oils, vinegars, and seasonings. With that in mind, feel free to play with the ingredients in this version: use grapeseed, nut, or vegetable oil in place of the extra virgin olive oil. Use sherry vinegar, balsamic vinegar, champagne vinegar, or flavored vinegar instead of the red wine vinegar. Use mustard powder or another variety of prepared mustard (or one of the mustards from the Mustards and Mayonnaises chapter in this book!) instead of the Dijon. And try different types of fresh or dry herbs and spices.

Makes 8 ounces

¼ cup red wine vinegar

½ teaspoon Dijon mustard

Pinch of kosher salt

Pinch of ground black pepper

¾ cup mild-flavored extra virgin olive oil

2 teaspoons finely chopped fresh herbs, such as parsley or thyme (optional)

In a small bowl, whisk together the vinegar, mustard, salt, and pepper until the mustard is completely incorporated into the vinegar and the salt has dissolved. While whisking constantly, slowly drizzle in the olive oil in a steady stream, until the mixture is smooth and emulsified. Stir in the herbs, if using, and season to taste with additional salt and pepper if desired. Use immediately or refrigerate for up to 1 week in a covered container. Whisk or shake in container to re-emulsify before using.

You can also make this dressing in a mason jar or a blender: simply add all the ingredients into the mason jar or blender container and shake or blend to combine.

Use It For

- Simple salad of mixed greens.
- Toss with cooked, cold pasta and Parmesan cheese for a pasta salad.
- Drizzle over poached salmon on a bed of greens.
- Marinate fish for a few minutes before sautéing.
- Toss with diced cucumbers and cherry tomatoes.

Maple Tarragon Vinaigrette

Mellow maple syrup is the perfect complement to the fresh, licorice-like flavor of fresh tarragon. This dressing is an elegant way to highlight an underrepresented herb.

Makes 4 ounces

¼ cup white wine vinegar

¾ teaspoon Dijon mustard

¼ teaspoon kosher salt

1 tablespoon maple syrup

¼ cup extra virgin olive oil

1 teaspoon minced fresh tarragon

In a small bowl, whisk together the vinegar, mustard, and salt until the mustard is completely incorporated into the vinegar and the salt has dissolved. Whisk in the maple syrup. While whisking constantly, slowly drizzle in the olive oil in a steady stream, until the mixture is smooth and emulsified. Stir in the tarragon and season to taste with additional salt if desired. Use immediately or refrigerate for up to 1 week in a covered container. Whisk or shake in container to re-emulsify before using.

Use It For

- Salad of mixed greens, dried cranberries, toasted walnuts, and goat cheese.
- Stir into diced grilled chicken and minced celery for a refreshing chicken salad.
- Drizzle over grilled peach slices.
- Brush on salmon before grilling or broiling.

Dilly Ranch Dressing

Buttermilk is my secret ingredient for creamy dressings—it is tangy, thick, and relatively healthy. (In this and any of the subsequent dressing recipes calling for buttermilk, you can use either low-fat or full-fat.) Keep a carton in your fridge and you'll not only always have the fixings for buttermilk pancakes, but you'll also be able to stir up a creamy dressing at a moment's notice. I like this herby dressing with fresh herbs, but you can also make it with dried if that's what you have on hand. Since dried herbs have a more concentrated flavor than fresh, you'll need about a teaspoon of each. If you do use dried herbs, it's a good idea to make the dressing an hour or more before you plan to serve it and let it sit in the refrigerator to allow the herby flavor to permeate the mixture.

Makes 8 ounces

¾ cup buttermilk

2 tablespoons mayonnaise

2 tablespoons sour cream
(low-fat or full-fat)

2 teaspoons minced fresh dill

2 teaspoons minced fresh chives

1 tablespoon minced fresh parsley

¼ teaspoon garlic powder

¼ teaspoon onion powder

¼ teaspoon kosher salt

In a small bowl, whisk together the buttermilk, mayonnaise, and sour cream. Add the dill, chives, parsley, garlic powder, onion powder, and salt and whisk to combine. Serve immediately if using fresh herbs or refrigerate for an hour or more if using dried herbs. The dressing will keep, covered, in the refrigerator for up to 2 days.

Use It For

- Salad of butter lettuce, cherry tomatoes, diced bell peppers, and sunflower seeds.
- Spread for turkey, cheddar, and sprouts or romaine wrap.
- Brush on chicken breasts before baking.
- Dip for crudité.
- Stir into mashed potatoes.
- Toss with diced cucumbers for a side salad.

Lemon Poppy Seed Buttermilk Dressing

Tart and refreshing, this dressing is light and creamy but without a lot of fat. If you're used to gloppy bottled dressing, you'll love the fresh flavor of this version.

Makes 4 ounces

½ teaspoon mustard powder

2 tablespoons buttermilk (low-fat or full-fat)

2 tablespoons fresh lemon juice

1 teaspoon granulated sugar

½ teaspoon kosher salt

2 tablespoons extra virgin olive oil

½ teaspoon minced shallot

1 teaspoon poppy seeds

In a small bowl, whisk together the mustard, buttermilk, lemon juice, sugar, and salt until smooth and the sugar and salt have dissolved. While whisking constantly, gradually drizzle in the olive oil until the mixture is emulsified. Stir in the shallot and poppy seeds. Use immediately or refrigerate, covered, for up to 2 hours. Whisk again to re-emulsify before serving.

Use It For

- Salad of butter lettuce, cherry tomatoes, and sunflower seeds.
- Drizzle over roasted fingerling potatoes.
- Dip for crudité.
- Toss with cooked rotini pasta, black olives, and diced red pepper.

Lime-Cumin Dressing

If you're having Mexican food for dinner and want to serve a salad, this is just the dressing for it. The lime and cumin flavor has a definitive Southwestern attitude. It's one of my favorite go-to dressings, easy to whip up with ingredients I nearly always have on hand.

Makes 4 ounces

¼ cup lime juice (2 limes)	½ teaspoon kosher salt	2 tablespoons extra virgin olive oil
½ teaspoon mustard powder	½ teaspoon ground cumin	
	1 tablespoon honey	

In a small bowl, whisk together the lime juice, mustard, salt, cumin, and honey until smooth. While whisking constantly, gradually drizzle in the olive oil until the mixture is emulsified. Use immediately or let sit at room temperature for up to 2 hours before using. Whisk to re-emulsify if needed.

Use It For

- Salad of butter lettuce or romaine, diced avocado, and toasted pumpkin seeds.
- Marinate tilapia before grilling for fish tacos.
- Stir into canned tuna or salmon and minced celery and spoon into the hollow of pitted avocado halves.
- Drizzle over grilled or sautéed shrimp.

Sesame-Ginger Dressing

Fresh ginger gives a kick to this Asian-style dressing. I make this dressing often to top salads that I serve with a stir-fry or with teriyaki-glazed salmon. If you make a lot of Asian dishes that require fresh ginger, consider buying a jar of grated ginger. It keeps for months in the refrigerator and is so much easier than peeling and grating a knob of fresh ginger.

Makes 4 ounces

½ teaspoon grated fresh ginger

½ teaspoon Dijon mustard

½ teaspoon honey

¼ cup rice vinegar

2 teaspoons sesame oil

¼ cup grapeseed oil or extra virgin olive oil

In a small bowl, whisk together the ginger, mustard, honey, and vinegar. Drizzle in the sesame oil and whisk to combine. While whisking constantly, drizzle in the grapeseed or olive oil until the mixture is emulsified. Use immediately or let sit at room temperature for up to 2 hours before using. Whisk to re-emulsify if needed.

Use It For

- Drizzle over cooked ramen noodles.
- Salad of mixed greens, daikon, avocado, and mung bean sprouts.
- Marinate salmon, tofu, or shrimp before grilling.
- Toss with cucumber slices and a handful of sesame seeds for an easy summer salad.
- Toss with stir-fried vegetables and brown rice.

Avocado Goddess Dressing

The first time I had green goddess dressing, with its pale green color, I thought it was going to be made with avocado, which is one of my all-time favorite foods. The dressing was good, but, alas, I learned that green goddess dressing is just a creamy dressing with herbs and sometimes anchovies. Although it was delicious, I decided to make the version that was in my mind. If you want to give this dressing more of a Southwestern feel, use lime juice instead of lemon juice and cilantro in place of the parsley.

Makes 8 ounces

1 small avocado, cut into chunks

1 tablespoon fresh lemon juice

2 tablespoons mayonnaise (low-fat or full-fat)

¾ cup buttermilk (low-fat or full-fat)

1 tablespoon minced fresh chives

1 tablespoon minced fresh parsley

¼ teaspoon garlic powder

¼ teaspoon kosher salt, or to taste

Place the avocado in a small bowl, drizzle the lemon juice over top, and add the mayonnaise. Using an immersion blender, blend the mixture until smooth. Add the buttermilk, chives, parsley, garlic powder, and salt, and blend until creamy and smooth. Serve immediately or store in a covered container in the refrigerator for up to 3 days.

Use It For
- Salad of romaine lettuce, chopped tomato, and slivered almonds.
- Dip for cucumber spears or baby carrots.
- Sauce for fish or chicken tacos.
- Condiment for a veggie burger with sliced avocado, tomato, and sprouts.
- Toss with chilled pasta, diced chicken, and black olives.

Caesar Dressing

I first shared my eggless Caesar dressing recipe in Ramen to the Rescue, *my first cookbook. It's inspired by the recipe my college friend HeeJai used to make. She put all the ingredients in a large zip-top bag to mash them all together and then tossed the salad right in the bag, but if you want to control the amount of dressing on your greens, make it the traditional way, in a bowl. This dressing is very robust—this small amount of dressing will dress enough greens for a salad for four.*

Makes about 5 ounces

1 medium clove garlic, minced

3 tinned anchovies, bones removed

3 tablespoons plain yogurt (low-fat or full-fat)

2 tablespoons fresh lemon juice

1 dash of Worcestershire sauce

¼ cup extra virgin olive oil

Kosher salt and black pepper

On a cutting board, mash the minced garlic with the side of a knife until it forms a paste. Place the anchovies on the board with the garlic and mash and chop them together until the garlic and anchovies are combined in a paste. Transfer the garlic-anchovy paste to a small bowl, and combine it with the yogurt, lemon juice, and Worcestershire sauce. While whisking constantly, drizzle in the olive oil until the mixture is emulsified. Season to taste with salt and pepper. Use immediately or store in the refrigerator for up to 1 day. You might need to stir the dressing again to mix the ingredients before using.

Use It For

- Salad with romaine leaves, grated Parmesan cheese, and garlicky croutons.
- Toss with hot or chilled pasta and kalamata olives.
- Marinate chicken before grilling.
- Dip for breadsticks.

Blue Cheese Dressing

This classic dressing is so elegant for a dinner party, but it also dresses down for game day wings. I like to buy good-quality blue cheese, but even the crumbles in the supermarket cheese case will work.

Makes about 10 to 12 ounces

2 tablespoons mayonnaise

1 cup buttermilk (low-fat or full-fat)

2 tablespoons minced fresh chives

1 tablespoon red wine vinegar

½ teaspoon garlic powder

Dash of Worcestershire sauce

⅔ cup crumbled blue cheese

Kosher salt and black pepper

In a bowl, combine the mayonnaise, buttermilk, chives, vinegar, garlic powder, and Worcestershire sauce, stirring with a whisk to combine. Using a spoon, stir in the blue cheese. Season to taste with salt and pepper. Serve immediately or store in a covered container in the refrigerator for up to 3 days.

Use It For

- Salad of iceberg wedge and crumbled bacon.
- Dip for hot wings and celery.
- Hamburger topping along with bacon and lettuce.
- Spread for a sandwich of roast beef, red onion, and sliced avocado.
- Mix with chopped chicken and walnuts for a chicken salad.

Orange-Miso Dressing

This dressing gets its thick, creamy consistency, not to mention its complex flavor, from miso, a thick paste of fermented soybeans and rice. You can find miso paste in the refrigerated section of most well-stocked supermarkets; it's usually near the tofu or the Asian ingredients. It's a bit pricey but it lasts forever in your refrigerator, so you'll always have it on hand to whip up this dressing or a bowl of miso soup.

Makes 4 ounces

2 tablespoons freshly squeezed orange juice (about ½ navel or Valencia)	1 tablespoon white miso paste ½ teaspoon Dijon mustard 3 tablespoons rice vinegar	2 tablespoons grapeseed or vegetable oil

In a small bowl, whisk together the orange juice, miso paste, and mustard until smooth and creamy. Gradually whisk in the vinegar until smooth and emulsified. While whisking, drizzle in the oil, whisking until it forms a thick, cohesive mixture.

Use immediately or store in the refrigerator for up to 3 days. You may need to whisk it to re-emulsify before serving.

Use It For

- An Asian slaw with chopped napa cabbage, roughly chopped cilantro, and crumbled uncooked ramen noodles.
- A salad of romaine lettuce, orange segments, avocado, and chilled poached shrimp.
- A sauce for seared scallops.
- A marinade for salmon or chicken breast before grilling.
- A dipping sauce for crudité, like carrots, red peppers, and peapods.

Ethnic & Specialty Condiments

Every international cuisine has its own set of condiments and sauces, which are as essential to those parts of the world as, say, ketchup is to us here in America. It's fun to explore condiments from around the world and start incorporating them into your cooking repertoire. Just as there are dozens of ways to use some of our favorite condiments, once you get to know the flavor profiles of ethnic condiments, chances are you'll find countless ways to use them as well.

In this chapter, I've also included a couple of specialty condiments, including bacon jam, cilantro pesto, and red pepper jelly—the latter is a classic pantry staple here in the South.

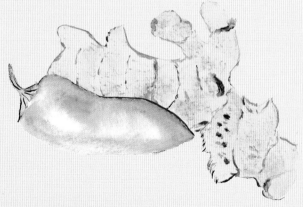

Sweet Chili Sauce

Thai cuisine is known for its balanced flavor profile: the ideal dish hits all the flavor points of spicy, sour, salty, and sweet. Sweet chili sauce, which hits nearly all these flavor aspects, is a topping found on the tables of nearly any Thai restaurant. With its syrupy sweetness coupled with a spicy kick, it's really addictive.

Makes 8 ounces

2 medium red jalapeño chile peppers, seeds and membranes removed, chopped	½ cup plus 2 teaspoons water, divided ¼ cup white vinegar ¼ cup granulated sugar	2 medium cloves garlic, minced Pinch of kosher salt 1 teaspoon cornstarch

You can remove all the seeds from the jalapeños or leave some for a spicier sauce. Place the jalapeños in a small saucepan with ½ cup water, vinegar, sugar, garlic, and salt. Bring to a simmer over medium heat. Reduce the heat to medium-low to maintain the simmer and cook for 15 minutes or until the peppers have softened. Transfer to a blender and pulse until the peppers are finely minced, or use an immersion blender right in the pan.

In a small bowl, combine the cornstarch with the remaining 2 teaspoons water and mix into a slurry. Return the pepper mix to the pan, stir in the cornstarch, and bring to a boil over medium-high heat. Boil for 1 minute or until thickened. Remove from heat and let cool to room temperature. Transfer to a covered container and keep refrigerated for up to 1 month.

Use It For

- Drizzle over brown rice and steamed broccoli.
- Brush on salmon fillets before grilling or broiling.
- Stir into ramen or other noodle soup.
- Dipping sauce for spring rolls or egg rolls.
- Glaze a pork roast.

Apricot Sweet and Sour Sauce

With this Chinese sauce, the name says it all, and it's a particular favorite among kids. But I stopped buying it by the jar when I saw that most versions were made with high fructose corn syrup. Instead, I make my own, using store-bought or homemade apricot preserves as the base. Fresh ginger adds extra dimension to this delicious sauce.

Makes 6 ounces

¾ cup apricot preserves

¼ cup rice vinegar

½ teaspoon grated fresh ginger

1 teaspoon soy sauce

1 teaspoon cornstarch

2 teaspoons water

In a saucepan or in the microwave, warm the preserves until they're soft and runny. Strain them through a fine-mesh colander into a bowl. You should end up with about ½ cup strained preserves. Discard the chunks of solids or save them for another use.

Place the strained preserves in a small saucepan and combine with the vinegar, ginger, and soy sauce. Bring to a simmer over medium heat. Place the cornstarch in a small ramekin or custard cup and combine with the water to make a slurry. Spoon the cornstarch slurry into the saucepan and bring the mixture to a boil over medium-high heat. Boil for 1 minute or until thickened. Let cool, then store in a covered container in the refrigerator for up to 1 month.

Use It For
- Toss with cooked chicken, green bell pepper, and pineapple chunks and serve over rice.
- Dipping sauce for egg rolls.
- Sauce for turkey meatballs.
- Sauce for stir-fried vegetables.
- Baste a chicken before grilling or broiling.

Tapenade

In the Provence region of France, tapenade is one of the most common condiments. It's a paste made from ground kalamata olives, anchovies, olive oil, and seasonings, and it has a robust, pungent flavor. This recipe calls for a few cloves of roasted garlic—you can use the garlic left over from making Roasted Garlic Olive Oil (page 70), or simply toss a few cloves with olive oil, wrap them in aluminum foil, and roast them for about 30 to 45 minutes in a 350°F oven until they're soft and mashable. If roasting the garlic cloves is too much trouble, just use one large fresh clove instead of three roasted ones. Use good-quality kalamata olives, such as those sold at a bulk olive bar in a gourmet food store. Since pitting olives is a tedious task, look for ones already pitted.

Makes 9 ounces

8 ounces pitted kalamata olives	3 medium cloves roasted garlic	½ teaspoon minced fresh thyme
2 tinned anchovies, bones removed	1 tablespoon capers	½ teaspoon grated lemon zest
	1 tablespoon fresh lemon juice	
	2 tablespoons extra virgin olive oil, plus more for storage	

In a food processor, combine the olives, anchovy fillets, garlic, and capers. Pulse to chop and combine the ingredients. Add the lemon juice, olive oil, thyme, and lemon zest and process until the mixture makes a chunky paste. Transfer the tapenade to a covered container, such as a glass jar, and pour a thin layer of olive oil over the top to help preserve the freshness. The tapenade will keep in the refrigerator for up to 2 weeks.

Use It For
- Spread on toasted baguette slices.
- Toss with hot pasta.
- Sandwich spread.
- Stir into potato salad.
- Condiment for grilled white fish or chicken breast.

Chimichurri

Chimichurri is Argentina's answer to Italy's pesto: a pungent, bright-tasting fresh herb sauce made with parsley, garlic, olive oil, and other ingredients. The Argentines use it on steak, either as a finishing sauce or a marinade. This version is quite thick and spreadable, like a pesto, but you can increase the liquid ingredients (the olive oil or vinegar) to make it a little more saucy if you plan to use it for a marinade or as a drizzle over finished dishes.

Makes 4 ounces

2 cups loosely packed Italian (flat-leaf) parsley

2 tablespoons fresh oregano

1 large clove garlic, minced

1 tablespoon minced shallot

$\frac{1}{4}$ teaspoon kosher salt, or to taste

$\frac{1}{8}$ teaspoon ground black pepper

$\frac{1}{4}$ teaspoon red pepper flakes, or to taste

2 tablespoons red wine vinegar

$\frac{1}{4}$ cup extra virgin olive oil

Place the parsley, oregano, garlic, shallot, salt, black pepper, and red pepper flakes in the bowl of a food processor. Pulse to finely chop. With the motor running, drizzle in the vinegar and olive oil until the mixture forms a paste. Season to taste with additional salt and pepper flakes if desired, or add more oil and/or vinegar if you want a looser sauce. Store, covered, in the refrigerator for up to 5 days. Bring to room temperature before using.

Use It For
- Condiment for steak.
- Marinade for chicken or beef.
- Spread or dip for French bread.
- Stir into black bean soup.
- Toss with pasta.

Cilantro-Almond Pesto

Cilantro's sharp flavor mellows in this pesto recipe, making a fresh-tasting alternative to the traditional basil version. Plus, I love any opportunity to use almonds in a savory recipe, since they're so good for you!

Makes 8 to 10 ounces

½ cup slivered blanched almonds (about 2 ounces)

3 cups loosely packed cilantro

½ cup grated Romano or Grana Padano cheese (about 2 ounces)

1 teaspoon lemon zest

½ cup extra virgin olive oil or grapeseed oil, or as needed

1 teaspoon lemon juice

¼ teaspoon kosher salt

Toast the almonds. Place them in a dry skillet and toast over medium heat, shaking or stirring frequently to prevent them from burning, until fragrant and lightly golden, about 3 to 5 minutes. Transfer to a plate or shallow bowl and let cool completely.

Place the cilantro, cheese, and lemon zest in a food processor and pulse several times to chop the cilantro. With the motor running, gradually drizzle in the oil, just enough to make a thin paste. Add the lemon juice and salt, and pulse once or twice to combine. Transfer to a covered container and store in the refrigerator for up to 5 days. (Pouring a very thin layer of oil over the top of your pesto before storing will help keep it from turning dark.)

Use It For

- Stir a dollop into posole or tortilla soup.
- Spread on a toasted baguette, top with crumbled queso fresco, and broil.
- Toss with hot pasta.
- Dip for baked flour tortilla chips.
- Stir into brown rice for a side dish or burrito filling.

Red Pepper Preserves

Red pepper jelly is one of those gourmet food items that you might never buy for yourself, but if you happen to get a jar as a gift, you'll wonder how you ever did without it. It's fantastic on just about everything and is a delicious helper for entertaining, since it can be used to make all sorts of appetizers. It's easy and quick to prepare, and a jar of the beautiful, jewel-toned jam makes a wonderful gift. Attach a tag with a list of ways the recipient can use it.

Makes 2 pints

2 pounds red bell peppers, seeds and membranes removed, roughly chopped (about 5 medium)	1 tablespoon kosher salt 1 cup white vinegar 1 tablespoon minced fresh ginger	1 teaspoon red pepper flakes 1 (1 ¾-ounce) package pectin 4 cups granulated sugar

Place the chopped bell pepper in the work bowl of a food processor and pulse until finely chopped. You should end up with about 4 cups of chopped bell pepper. Transfer to a fine-mesh colander suspended over a bowl or the sink and sprinkle with the salt, stirring to mix it in. Let sit for 3 to 4 hours to allow excess liquid to drain. Rinse the salt off the bell pepper and give the colander a few shakes to drain off excess water.

Sterilize jars and let sit in hot water to keep jars hot until needed (see canning and sterilizing instructions on page 118).

Place the bell pepper, vinegar, ginger, and red pepper flakes in a medium saucepan and stir in the pectin. Bring to a rolling boil over high heat, stirring frequently. When the mixture is boiling, stir in the sugar all at once and return the mixture to a boil, stirring frequently. When the mixture is at a rolling boil, let it cook for 1 minute, stirring constantly. The mixture should thicken and get glassy-looking. After 1 minute, remove from the heat, skim off any foam that accumulated on the surface, and ladle into hot pint jars, leaving about ¼ inch headspace. Process in a boiling water canner for 10 minutes. Let the jars cool completely.

Use It For
- Pour over a block of cream cheese and serve with crackers as a spread.
- Mix with ricotta cheese for a dip.
- Brush onto raw chicken before baking.
- Use as a condiment for roast pork.

Teriyaki Sauce

The word "teriyaki" actually refers more to the Japanese technique of grilling or broiling foods than to the sauce itself. But the sweet-tangy sauce has become synonymous with the word. It's easy enough to make at home, and once you do make a batch, you'll find that it is so delicious you'll want to use it for more than just brushing on meats you're grilling.

Makes 6 ounces

¼ cup soy sauce

½ cup granulated sugar

1 tablespoon mirin (Japanese wine) or dry sherry

½ cup rice vinegar

2 teaspoons tomato paste

1 teaspoon grated fresh ginger

¼ teaspoon garlic powder

¼ teaspoon onion powder

2 teaspoons cornstarch

1 tablespoon water

In a small saucepan, combine the soy sauce, sugar, mirin or sherry, vinegar, tomato paste, ginger, garlic powder, and onion powder. Bring to a simmer over medium-high heat, then reduce the heat to low and simmer, uncovered, for 5 minutes to allow the flavors to develop. In a small ramekin or custard cup, combine the cornstarch and water, stirring until it's a slurry. Add the cornstarch mixture to the mixture in the pan and increase the heat to medium-high to bring it to a boil. Boil the mixture for 1 minute or until thickened. Store, covered, in the refrigerator for up to 1 week.

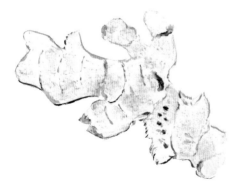

Use It For
- Brush on chicken, beef, pork, or fish before grilling or broiling.
- Mix with stir-fried noodles and vegetables.
- Brush on kebabs for grilling.
- Combine with chicken thighs in the slow cooker.
- Toss with cubed seared tofu and serve on rice.

Hoisin Sauce

Hoisin sauce is China's form of barbecue sauce and, like American barbecue sauce, is similarly complex, with sweet, tangy, salty, and spicy elements. It can be used in much the same way as barbecue sauce, or it can add body and dimension to other Asian sauces. Look for miso in the refrigerated section of well-stocked supermarkets or Asian grocers—it'll probably be with the tofu. If you can't find it, creamy peanut butter is a good substitute.

Makes about 4 ounces

¼ cup miso paste

2 tablespoons soy sauce

1 teaspoon molasses

2 teaspoons granulated sugar

1 tablespoon plus 1 teaspoon rice vinegar

1 teaspoon sesame oil

⅛ teaspoon garlic powder

¼ teaspoon red pepper flakes

In a small bowl, combine the miso paste, soy sauce, molasses, sugar, rice vinegar, sesame oil, garlic powder, and red pepper flakes. Stir until smooth. The sauce will keep, covered, in the refrigerator for up to 2 weeks.

Use It For
- Brush on pork shoulder or brisket before grilling.
- Mix with chunks of beef, pork, or chicken in a slow cooker.
- Condiment for moo shu pork.
- Dipping sauce for spring rolls or fried filled wontons.
- Ingredient in stir-fry sauce.

Caramelized Onion Chutney

I've always marveled at the transformation of onions when they caramelize, going from sharp and pungent and crunchy to something silky, sweet, and complex. This recipe makes beautiful use of the alchemy, hitting all the taste sensations of sweet, salty, spicy, and sour.

Makes about 9 ounces

1 tablespoon grapeseed or other neutral-flavored oil	2 tablespoons brown sugar	¼ teaspoon red pepper flakes
1½ pounds sweet onions, cut in half and thinly sliced crosswise (about 3 large)	½ cup raisins	¼ teaspoon kosher salt
	¼ cup cider vinegar	

Heat the oil in a large skillet over medium-low heat. Add the onions and sugar, stir to combine, and cook, uncovered, stirring occasionally, for 60 to 75 minutes, until the onions are very soft, dark golden brown, and sweet.

Stir in the raisins, vinegar, red pepper flakes, and salt and sauté for about 5 minutes, stirring occasionally, until the vinegar cooks off and the raisins soften. Let cool, then store in a covered container in the refrigerator for up to 1 week.

Use It For
- On toasted baguette slices.
- Spoon over cream cheese or goat cheese for an appetizer spread.
- In grilled cheese sandwiches.
- On brie wrapped in puff pastry and baked.
- Condiment with roast pork or chicken.

Pear Chutney

For this chutney, choose barely ripe pears that are firm but not rock-hard. Too-ripe pears will not hold their shape and texture during the cooking process. I like to use Bosc or Bartlett pears, but just about any variety will work.

Makes 16 ounces

1 tablespoon butter

½ cup minced yellow onion (about ½ medium)

1 pound unpeeled pears, chopped (about 3 medium)

1 tablespoon brown sugar

¼ cup cider vinegar

½ cup raisins

1 teaspoon grated fresh ginger

½ teaspoon ground cinnamon

¼ teaspoon kosher salt

⅛ teaspoon ground red pepper

In a medium saucepan, melt the butter over medium heat. Add the onion and cook for about 5 minutes or until lightly browned. Add the pears, brown sugar, vinegar, raisins, ginger, cinnamon, salt, and ground red pepper. Cook, stirring occasionally, for 10 minutes or until the pears have softened but still hold their shape. Let the mixture cool, then transfer to a lidded container and refrigerate for up to 1 week.

Use It For

- Condiment for roast chicken or pork.
- On crostini, topped with blue cheese and broiled.
- On a cheese plate with sharp cheddar, smoked gouda, or brie.
- Mix with cooked quinoa.
- Spoon into a casserole dish, top with buttered cracker crumbs and bake until hot for a savory crumble.

Mango Chutney

This is my twist on the classic Indian condiment, a sweet and tart way to enjoy the tropical flavor and juicy texture of mango. For instructions on the best way to cut a mango, see page 67.

Makes 12 ounces

½ cup brown sugar

½ cup cider vinegar

½ cup white vinegar

½ cup chopped yellow onion (about ½ medium)

1 medium clove garlic, minced

2 cups mangoes, cut into small chunks (about 2 medium)

1 cup raisins

2 teaspoons grated fresh ginger

1 teaspoon yellow mustard seeds

Red pepper flakes, to taste

¼ teaspoon kosher salt, or to taste

In a medium saucepan, combine the sugar, cider vinegar, and white vinegar. Bring to a simmer over medium heat and simmer until the sugar has dissolved, about 3 to 4 minutes. Add the onion, garlic, mango, raisins, ginger, and mustard seeds and simmer for 15 to 20 minutes or until the mixture is thick and syrupy. Stir in the red pepper flakes and season with the salt. Let the mixture cool, then transfer to a lidded container and refrigerate for up to 1 week.

Use It For
- Stir into curried chicken salad.
- Condiment for roast chicken or pork.
- On a cheese plate.
- Spoon over a block of cream cheese for an appetizer.

Bacon Jam

Among the condiments at a fancy burger place in my city is bacon jam, a sticky-sweet and salty topping that is particularly yummy on a turkey burger. My version combines the smoky saltiness of bacon, the tanginess of apples, and the sweetness of slow-cooked red onions. Because the jam contains meat, don't try canning it as you would a fruit jam. Instead, keep it in the refrigerator for several weeks. If whitish congealed fat appears, just spoon out what you'll need into a glass dish and warm it for a few seconds in the microwave.

Makes 16 ounces

1 pound thick-cut bacon, cut crosswise into thin strips

1 large red onion, quartered from stem to end and thinly sliced

2 medium cloves garlic, thinly sliced

¾ cup apple cider vinegar, plus more if needed

¾ cup brown sugar

Place the bacon in a large, heavy-bottom saucepan or skillet. Cook over medium-high heat, stirring frequently with a wooden spoon, until dark and crisp, about 15 minutes. Spoon all but 2 tablespoons of the fat into a heatproof bowl and reserve in case you need it. Add the onion and cook over medium heat until very soft and dark, about 15 minutes. Add more fat, a teaspoon or two at a time, if needed to keep the onion from burning. Add the garlic and cook for 1 minute, stirring constantly.

Pour the vinegar into the pan all at once and stir, using the spoon to scrape any stuck-on bits from the bottom of the pan. Stir in the sugar, reduce the heat to low, and simmer, uncovered, until nearly all the liquid has reduced and the mixture is thick and syrupy, about 30 to 35 minutes. Spoon into a lidded container and store in the refrigerator for up to 3 weeks.

Use It For
- Spread on toast for a sprout and avocado sandwich.
- Slather on a toasted English muffin and top with a poached egg.
- Mix with sour cream for a dip or cream cheese for a spread for crackers.
- Burger topping along with blue cheese and crisp Romaine lettuce.
- In a grilled cheese sandwich.
- Dollop on endive leaves for an appetizer.

Sweet Sauces & Spreads

Condiments aren't just for savory foods—if you think about it, there is a wealth of condiments available for adding flavor, color, texture, contrast, and visual interest to sweet breakfast dishes, desserts, and snacks. Use them whenever you want to add a little something extra to a dish.

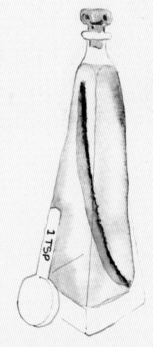

Peanut Butter

When I realized how quick, easy, and inexpensive peanut butter is to make at home, I stopped buying the store-bought versions. And, yes, it does indeed get just as creamy as your favorite commercial brand, if you have patience and a decent food processor.

Makes about 8 ounces

1 ¾ cups roasted, skinless, unsalted peanuts (about 8 ounces)

1 tablespoon peanut oil or grapeseed oil, or other neutral-tasting oil

½ teaspoon honey
½ teaspoon kosher salt

Place the peanuts in the work bowl of a food processor. Process for about 30 seconds, until the nuts are ground into a powder, roughly the texture of cornmeal. When the contents begin looking clumpy, drizzle in the oil, honey, and salt through the feed tube. Continue processing until the mixture is very smooth, about 1 to 2 minutes. Transfer to a covered container and keep in the refrigerator for up to a month. Stir any separated oil back into the peanut butter as necessary and, if the peanut butter hardens in the refrigerator, let it sit out for 10 minutes or so before using.

Use It For
- Peanut butter and jelly sandwiches.
- Peanut butter cookies.
- Stir into a bowl of hot ramen.
- Spread on apple slices.
- Spread on celery spears and top with raisins.

PEANUT BUTTER

Almond Butter

Delicately flavored almonds have myriad health benefits, from protecting the body against cardiovascular diseases and diabetes, to increasing your energy levels and helping you to lose weight. It's easy to make your own almond butter, and far less expensive: this 1-cup batch costs less than $3 to make, while jars of nut butter sell at health food stores for upward of $6. Whip up a batch of this almond butter and use in place of peanut butter for a mellow-tasting, nutrient-packed treat. Toasting the almonds before processing gives them a more pronounced flavor.

Makes about 8 ounces

½ pound blanched slivered almonds

¼ cup almond oil, grapeseed oil, or other neutral-tasting oil

1 tablespoon honey

½ teaspoon kosher salt

Preheat the oven to 350°F. Spread the almonds on a sheet pan and toast in the oven, stirring occasionally, until the nuts are fragrant and lightly browned. Be sure to watch the nuts carefully to keep them from burning. Let cool.

Add the cooled nuts to the bowl of a food processor. Process the nuts into a cornmeal-textured flour, and then they'll gradually break down into a clumpy mass. While the motor is running, gradually drizzle in the oil and continue to process until the nuts are a mostly smooth, spreadable consistency. Stop the food processor to scrape down or redistribute the mixture as necessary. Add the honey and salt and process to combine. The almond butter will keep, covered and refrigerated, for 1 to 2 months. Stir any separated oil back into the almond butter as necessary, and if it becomes hard in the refrigerator, let it sit out for 10 minutes or so before using.

Use It For

- In place of peanut butter for peanut butter cookies.
- Spread onto pear slices.
- Slathered onto toast.
- Blended into smoothies.
- Pureed in butternut squash or carrot soups.

Chocolate Almond Spread

I knew I had to include a recipe similar to Nutella, the chocolate hazelnut spread, in this book. Nutella was developed in Italy in the 1940s to stretch the cocoa being rationed during World War II with readily available hazelnuts. Today, the cost of hazelnuts far outpaces that of cocoa, so my version uses almonds. This spread is soft and creamy at room temperature but hardens in the fridge. Let it sit out awhile before using it, or scoop out a bit and soften it in the microwave.

Makes about 11 ounces

6-ounce bar semisweet chocolate, chopped

1 tablespoon vegetable oil, grapeseed oil, or other neutral-tasting oil

½ cup warmed milk

1 cup blanched slivered almonds (about 4 ounces)

Pinch of kosher salt

½ teaspoon vanilla extract

Fill the bottom of a double boiler with a few inches of water (or create a double boiler; see Mixing Bowls, page 5), bring the water to a simmer over medium heat, and then reduce the heat to low to maintain the simmer. Add the chocolate to the double boiler insert and heat, stirring frequently, until the chocolate is completely melted and smooth. Add the oil and the milk, stirring until the mixture is combined. Turn the heat off, but leave the melted chocolate sitting in the double boiler.

Place the almonds in the work bowl of a food processor and process until finely ground and clumpy, like wet sand. Add the melted chocolate and the salt and process until the mixture is smooth and creamy. Add the vanilla and pulse to mix it in completely. Scrape the chocolate spread into a lidded container and refrigerate for up to 2 weeks.

Use It For
- Filling between cake layers.
- Spread on toast or graham crackers.
- Mix into buttercream frosting.
- Heat until syrupy and drizzle over ice cream.
- Filling for crepes.

Hot Fudge Sauce

I couldn't do a chapter of sweet condiments without my favorite ice cream topping! This version is very rich and dark. If you want it sweeter, you could add a little more sugar. Use good-quality cocoa powder and don't neglect the instructions to sift it or you'll wind up with lumpy sauce.

Makes about 12 ounces

1 (12-ounce) can evaporated milk

½ cup light corn syrup

½ cup granulated sugar

2 tablespoons all-purpose flour

½ cup sifted unsweetened cocoa powder

Pinch of kosher salt

1 teaspoon vanilla extract

Add the evaporated milk, corn syrup, and sugar to a medium saucepan and bring to a simmer over medium-low heat, stirring frequently. When the mixture reaches a simmer, whisk in the flour and continue whisking for 3 to 4 minutes, until the mixture has thickened into a gravy-like consistency.

Whisk in the cocoa powder and simmer, whisking constantly, for an additional 3 to 4 minutes, until the sauce is smooth and thick. Stir in the salt. Remove from the heat and stir in the vanilla. Use immediately or let cool, transfer to a covered container, and refrigerate for up to 1 week. You will need to reheat the sauce on the stove or in the microwave before using it.

Use It For

- Hot fudge sundaes.
- Filling for mini tarts.
- Blend into a milkshake.
- As a chilled spread on toast or graham crackers.
- As a chilled frosting for brownies or cookies.
- Drizzle over cheesecake.

Caramel Sauce

Don't be afraid of making real, honest-to-goodness caramel sauce. The process of caramelizing sugar can be daunting, but the result is well worth the effort! An uncoated stainless steel saucepan is preferable, as the dark finish of a nonstick pan makes it difficult to watch the color of the sugar as it caramelizes. Best of all is a saucier pan—the sloped sides allow for even cooking and stirring. Caramel can go quickly from perfect to burnt, so keep a close eye on the pan.

Makes about 14 ounces

1 cup sugar	1 cup heavy cream	1 teaspoon vanilla extract
1 tablespoon corn syrup	2 tablespoons butter	Sea salt, to taste
1 tablespoon water		

In a heavy-bottom saucepan, combine the sugar, corn syrup, and water over medium-low heat. Heat the mixture until the sugar melts. Reduce the heat to low so that it's just barely simmering and watch closely, but don't stir. The mixture will take about 15 to 20 minutes to turn amber brown.

Meanwhile, heat the heavy cream in a small saucepan over medium-low heat or in the microwave. When the sugar mixture is amber brown, remove it from the heat and add the cream and butter, stirring constantly until the mixture is syrupy and smooth. Stir in the vanilla extract and season to taste with the salt. The caramel sauce will keep, covered, in the refrigerator for up to 2 weeks.

Variation:

Salted Caramel Sauce

To make salted caramel sauce, simply stir in flaky sea salt (1 teaspoon or more to taste) when the sauce has cooled to lukewarm. I prefer Maldon, which has large flakes.

Use It For
- Spoon over ice cream.
- Stir into hot cocoa or coffee drinks.
- Dipping sauce for apple slices.
- Drizzle over warmed apple pie.
- Stir into brownie batter for turtle brownies.

Berry Sauce

You can use just-picked berries or frozen ones in this versatile, fresh-tasting sauce. Use any combination of berries that you have on hand, or focus on the flavor of one or two varieties. I like a mix of blackberries, strawberries, blueberries, and raspberries—you might even be able to find bags of frozen berries that contain a blend. You can save the berry solids that you strain out the sauce for a fresh (if seedy) fruit spread.

Makes about 16 ounces

5 cups fresh or frozen berries (about 1 ½ pounds)	¼ cup sugar	2 tablespoons lemon juice (optional)

In a saucepan, combine the berries and sugar over medium-low heat, stirring occasionally. Bring to a simmer, then reduce the heat to medium-low to maintain a simmer. Cook, stirring occasionally and breaking up chunks of berries with your spoon, for 15 to 20 minutes, until the berries have broken down and the juice has thickened.

Strain into a bowl through a fine-mesh sieve or a food mill fitted with the finest disc. If desired, stir in the lemon juice to give the sauce some tartness. Use immediately or store, covered, in the refrigerator for up to 1 week.

Use It For

- Topping for ice cream.
- Drizzle over pound cake or angel food cake.
- Swirl on plain or vanilla yogurt.
- Write or draw patterns on a white plate for a restaurant-quality plated dessert.
- Dollop on pancakes or waffles.
- Whip into frosting, a few tablespoons at a time, for flavor and color.

Crunchy-Shell Chocolate Sauce

I used to love Magic Shell ice cream topping as a kid, and last summer on a whim I bought some for my kids. But one look at the label (sugar, sunflower oil, and coconut oil are the top three ingredients) made me wonder if I could make my own. This version is the closest I've come, and it's even more delicious than the store-bought variety.

Makes about 16 ounces

12 ounces semisweet chocolate, in chips or a bar chopped into chunks (about 2 cups)	1 ¼ cups warmed heavy cream	2 tablespoons light corn syrup

In a heavy-bottom saucepan, melt the chocolate over medium-low heat, stirring often and taking care not to scorch it on the bottom of the pan. When it's completely melted, stir in the cream and corn syrup. Keep stirring until the ingredients mix together into a smooth, creamy sauce. Spoon immediately over ice cream and let sit for a few moments before eating to allow a hard shell to form. The sauce will keep, covered, in the refrigerator up to 3 days. Before using it, melt it in a saucepan on the stove or heat it in the microwave.

Use It For
- Topping for ice cream.
- Pipe onto a chilled dessert plate to make a design or write a message.
- Dip strawberries in the melted sauce and chill until firm.
- Ladle warm sauce over small pieces of pound cake and refrigerate until firm to make petits fours.

Dulce de Leche

Translated from Spanish as "sweet milk" or "milk jam," this South American treat has become a favored flavoring for everything from ice cream to coffee drinks to cake. One popular legend about the origin of dulce de leche claims that it was the happy result of an accident in Buenos Aires: a woman boiling sweet milk for some soldiers during a war forgot about her pot on the stove, returning to find the milk had boiled down to a thick, dark substance. Other South American and Central American countries have their own versions and try to lay claim to its creation. However—and wherever—it was first made, it's a wonderful treat that is easy to make at home and requires just two ingredients and a couple of hours hanging around the stove.

Makes about 8 ounces

1 (14½-ounce) can sweetened condensed milk	½ teaspoon vanilla extract

Spoon the condensed milk into the top of a double boiler (or create a double boiler; see Mixing Bowls, page 5) and set aside. Fill the bottom of the double boiler with a few inches of water and bring to a simmer over medium heat, then reduce the heat to low or medium-low to maintain the simmer. Place the insert into the base, and cook the milk over the simmering water, stirring every 20 to 30 minutes. Scrape down the sides of the insert as needed and keep an eye on the water level in the base adding more when needed so it doesn't boil dry. After about 1½ to 2 hours, the milk will be very thick and dark golden and will have a caramel flavor. Transfer the dulce de leche to a heatproof container and stir in the vanilla extract. The dulce de leche will keep, covered, in the refrigerator for up to 3 weeks.

Use It For

- Flavoring for homemade ice cream.
- Filling for sandwich cookies or mini tart shells.
- Spread on toast or crackers.
- Dipping sauce for apple wedges.
- Drizzle on ice cream.
- Filling between the layers of a cake.

Wet Walnuts

Right under the Brooklyn Bridge, on the Brooklyn side of the East River, there's a little ice cream shop that I used to visit after a walk across the bridge. They had the creamiest, most delicious ice cream, made all the yummier with a generous dousing of walnuts in a sweet syrup. This recipe is my homage to what became my favorite summertime treat.

Makes 8 ounces

1 cup roughly chopped walnuts (about 3 ounces)	¼ cup light corn syrup 2 tablespoons maple syrup	Pinch of kosher salt

Toast the walnuts. Place them in a dry skillet and toast over medium heat, shaking or stirring frequently to prevent them from burning, until fragrant and lightly golden, about 3 to 5 minutes. Transfer to a plate or shallow bowl and let cool completely.

In a lidded container, stir together the corn syrup and maple syrup. Stir in the walnuts (it's okay to do so before they cool) and the salt. Store, covered, in the refrigerator for up to 2 weeks. If the mixture is too dense to pour, let it come to room temperature or microwave it for 20 seconds before serving.

Use It For
- Spoon over yogurt.
- Spread on a wheel of brie, wrap in pastry, and bake for an appetizer.
- Topping for ice cream or frozen yogurt.
- On pancakes, waffles, or French toast.
- Swirl into brownie batter before baking.

Luscious Lemon Curd

I first fell in love with lemon curd as a child, when my mother would take me on a special outing for afternoon tea. We'd perch on sofas in the dining room of the Ritz-Carlton, sipping tea and slathering scones with lemon curd and clotted cream just like proper English ladies. Now that I've learned how easy it is to make lemon curd from scratch, I don't have to make reservations at the Ritz to indulge myself.

Makes about 12 ounces

2 whole eggs	⅔ cup sugar	½ cup fresh lemon juice
2 egg yolks	1 teaspoon lemon zest	3 tablespoons butter

Fill the bottom of a double boiler with a few inches of water (or create a double boiler; see Mixing Bowls, page 5), bring the water to a simmer over medium heat, and then reduce the heat to low to maintain the simmer. Fit a fine-mesh sieve over a medium bowl and set aside.

With the double boiler insert off the heat, add the eggs and yolks to the insert and whisk until smooth. Then whisk in the sugar, lemon zest, and lemon juice. Over low heat, put the insert into the base and continue whisking over the simmering water for about 10 minutes, until the mixture thickens enough so that a spoon dragged through the mixture leaves an indentation. Remove from the heat. Pour the curd into the sieve, stirring and pressing with a wooden spoon or a spatula to push the mixture through the mesh, leaving behind any lumps of scrambled egg or large pieces of zest. Stir the butter into the curd while it's still hot. Let cool, then transfer to a lidded container, press plastic wrap onto the surface of the cooled curd to avoid a "skin" forming, and refrigerate for up to 1 week.

Use It For
- Filling between cake layers.
- Drizzle over slices of pound cake or angel food cake.
- Spoon on shortcake and berries and top with whipped cream.
- Swirl into plain or vanilla yogurt.
- Drizzle over vanilla or fruit-flavored ice cream.
- Spread on freshly baked scones and top with clotted cream or whipped cream.
- Mix with mascarpone for a delicious fruit dip.

Cherry-Fig Compote

Dried fruit is simmered in fruity pinot noir, which adds complexity and depth to this condiment, equally at home in sweet and savory dishes. You can experiment with different dried fruits— dried apricots or cranberries, for instance. Or try using a sweet white wine like Riesling instead of pinot.

Makes about 12 ounces

1 ½ cups pinot noir	1 cup quartered dried figs	1 cinnamon stick
1 cup roughly chopped dried cherries	1 tablespoon honey (2 tablespoons if cherries are tart)	2 star anise
		Pinch of sea salt

In a saucepan, combine the wine, cherries, figs, honey, cinnamon stick, and star anise. Bring to a simmer over medium heat, then reduce the heat to medium-low and simmer for 20 to 25 minutes, until the dried fruit has plumped and the liquid is reduced and syrupy. Stir in the salt. Serve warm. The compote will keep in a covered container in the refrigerator for up to 3 days.

Use It For

- Condiment for roast pork or duck breast.
- On a cheese plate, especially with bold-flavored cheeses like blue cheese or Parmesan.
- Topping for rice pudding.
- Stir into oatmeal.

Tropical Pineapple-Cashew Compote

Sunny flavors like pineapple, coconut, and cashews combine in this compote, which is delicious either warm or chilled. Check out the instructions for cutting a pineapple in the Tropical Salsa recipe (page 66). You can make this recipe into a savory compote by sautéing about $\frac{1}{4}$ cup diced yellow onion in the saucepan before adding the pineapple and finishing the dish with a pinch of red pepper flakes.

Makes about 16 ounces

1 cup roughly chopped cashews (about 4 ounces)	2 tablespoons brown sugar	Pinch of kosher salt
$3\frac{1}{2}$ cups chopped fresh pineapple	$\frac{1}{2}$ cup water	$\frac{1}{4}$ cup sweetened coconut flakes
	1 to 2 tablespoons rum (optional)	

Toast the cashews. Place them in a dry skillet and toast over medium heat, shaking or stirring frequently to prevent them from burning, until fragrant and lightly golden, about 3 to 5 minutes. Transfer to a plate or shallow bowl and let cool completely.

In a saucepan over medium heat, combine the pineapple, sugar, water, and rum if using, and bring to a simmer. Reduce heat to medium-low and cook, uncovered, stirring occasionally, for about 15 minutes, until the pineapple has softened and is a little dark. With a slotted spoon, transfer the pineapple to a large bowl, leaving the juice behind. Simmer the remaining juice in the pan until syrupy, 1 to 2 minutes. Pour the juice over the pineapple in the bowl and season the mixture lightly with the salt. Stir in the cashews and coconut flakes. Serve warm or chilled. The compote will keep in a covered container in the refrigerator for up to 3 days.

Use It For

- Spoon over ice cream or frozen yogurt.
- Serve over sautéed chicken thighs and brown rice.
- Mix with cooked quinoa or couscous for a tropical salad.
- Topping for rice pudding.

Appendix

Food Safety and Canning

When you prepare foods that won't be eaten right away, it's important to take precautions to preserve them so they remain safe and free from bacteria that could sicken people.

Disclaimer: Please note that although every effort has been made to provide information about food safety and canning and other food preservation techniques in this book, there is always a risk of foodborne illness when preparing any type of food. Ulysses Press and the author are not responsible for any illness that results from preparing and eating the fare featured in these recipes.

These tips and instructions will ensure optimal results when you're canning pickles, jelly, and other foods. I highly recommend the following resources, which I used as references for my recipes and methods:

Ball Blue Book: Guide to Home Canning, Freezing & Dehydration
I used the 1995 edition, but there are several updated editions available in bookstores and online. The Ball brand is now owned by Jarden Consumer Products.

National Center for Home Food Preservation
Established in conjunction with the University of Georgia and Alabama A&M University, this center serves as a resource for consumer information about all aspects of food preservation. It contains detailed instructions, tutorials, slideshows, recipes, and other materials to help educate the public about the various ways to "put up" food. Visit their website at nchfp.uga.edu.

PickYourOwn.org
Don't be put off by the "homegrown" look of this website. In addition to offering a state-by-state directory of farms across the country where you can pick your own fruits and vegetables, it has instructions and recipes for canning produce, a list of sources for buying canning supplies, and a list of recommended canning books.

Canning Tips

1. Start with fresh, good-quality ingredients. I prefer to buy organic ingredients wherever possible. Check produce before you use it, discarding (or cutting away) any items that are bruised, moldy, or otherwise damaged.

2. Follow directions exactly. Many of the recipes require a certain proportion of, say, vinegar or sugar, in order not only to yield the proper flavor and consistency, but also to keep the food properly preserved. What's more, it's also crucial to adhere to the cooking and processing times indicated to make sure that your recipes will be successful and the jars properly sealed.

3. Keep it clean. An important aspect of canning and preserving is to make sure that harmful bacteria don't get into the food, where it has the chance to multiply and contaminate the jarred goods. Keep your work surfaces scrupulously clean, sterilize everything you can, and wash your hands often with soap and hot water.

4. Make adjustments for altitude. The processing times listed in this book are for altitudes of around 1,000 feet. If you are at a higher or lower altitude, you can find information online for how to change processing time.

Canning Equipment

This is the basic equipment you'll need to can the pickles and preserves in this book. If you get the canning bug, as I have, you'll likely find yourself adding to your arsenal whenever you come across new tools and gadgets. All the canning recipes in this book are made using a boiling water canner, as opposed to a steam pressure canner.

Boiling Water Canner: Most boiling water canners are basically large lidded pots, made of coated steel or aluminum, and include a rack to hold the jars. The rack can be suspended from the sides of the canner and, once the jars are added, lowered into the boiling water.

Jars: The safest jars for home canning are glass jars with a two-part lid: a flat metal lid with a rubber interior ring that creates the seal and a threaded metal band that holds the lid in place. While the glass jars and the metal bands (provided they're not bent, rusty, or otherwise damaged) can be reused as long as they're still in good condition, the flat lids can be used only once, as they will not create a good seal a second time. The lids and bands are sold separately, so they're easy to replace without having to buy new jars. Jars come in several sizes: quarter pint ($\frac{1}{2}$ cup), half pint (1 cup), pint (2 cups), and quart (4 cups). The larger jars usually come in wide- or narrow-mouth styles. I prefer the wider mouth jars as they're easier to fill and wash.

Utensils: Although you can make do with equipment you already have on hand, certain canning-specific tools will make the job easier: a jar lifter looks like a pair of tongs, but with wide, curved ends (usually coated in grippy rubber) that can securely grip jars to lift them out of the boiling water canner. A jar funnel, with a wide mouth that fits perfectly into jars, makes the task of filling hot jars easier and neater. A lid wand is a long plastic handle with a magnetized tip, which makes it easy to lift hot lids and bands out of the water in which they're being heated or sterilized.

A canning kit, which includes the boiling water canning pot and rack as well as a selection of utensils, is a good starting point for beginners.

Sterilizing Jars

According to *Ball Blue Book*, jars do not need to be sterilized unless they will be processed in the boiling water canner for less than 10 minutes. Regardless of processing time, before filling jars I usually sterilize all the jars I'll be using, including ones being used for refrigerated condiments.

To sterilize jars, first wash them well with detergent and hot water and rinse well to remove every trace of detergent. Place jars in a large saucepan or pot and fill the pot with enough water to submerge the jars. Bring the water to a boil and boil for 10 minutes. Do not sterilize jars in the dishwasher, as this is an unreliable method. The lids should not be sterilized as the prolonged contact with boiling water can damage the rubberized sealing surface and the metal bands do not need to be sterilized either.

Canning Basics

These basic instructions for canning can be used for the recipes in the Pickles & Relishes chapter (page 49) and the Red Pepper Preserves (page 95).

Set Up: Fill a boiling water canner about halfway with water (make sure that your largest jar will be completely submerged with at least 1 inch of water overhead) and bring to a boil. Suspend the rack over the water. Heat another pot of water and sterilize the jars if needed. Turn off the heat and keep the jars, along with the lids and bands, in hot water until ready to fill.

Make Recipe: When the jars have been sterilized or heated for at least 10 minutes and the water in the canner is at the boiling point, prepare your recipe according to instructions. Have all equipment ready to immediately fill and process the jars.

Fill Jars: The rule in canning is that hot food goes in hot jars and cold food goes in cold jars, which prevents jars from breaking. In this book, the canning recipes are all for hot food in hot jars. Take the jars out one at a time with a jar lifter or a pair of rubber-tipped tongs, shaking off the excess liquid. Ladle in the hot food using a funnel and leaving the recommended amount of headspace. Headspace refers to the distance remaining between the surface of the food and the top of the jar. It's important to use the proper amount of headspace depending on what sort of recipe you're preparing. Too little headspace, particularly for food that expands, might cause food to seep under the lid and prevent a proper seal. Too much headspace could cause too much air to remain in the jar, also preventing a proper seal. The general rule is $\frac{1}{4}$-inch headspace for jams, jellies, pickles, and relishes and $\frac{1}{2}$-inch headspace for acidic fruits and tomatoes.

Use a chopstick, skewer, or canning spatula to gently stir or poke the contents of the jar to remove any air bubbles. You can also tap the jar a few times against the counter to encourage bubbles to rise (use a clean towel or an oven mitt to hold the hot jar).

Place the Lid: Use a clean, damp cloth to wipe the rim and threads of the jar to make sure that nothing will interfere with the seal. Then place the lid on the jar rim, centering it so that the rubbery sealing compound is in contact with the glass rim. Place the band on the lid and screw it just until you encounter resistance.

Process: As you fill the jars, place them on the rack suspended over the water in the canner. Once all the jars are filled and placed on the rack, carefully lower the rack into the water. The water should cover the jars by 1 to 2 inches—you can add hot water from the pot that held the hot jars if you need more water. Put the canner lid in place and bring the water to a rolling boil over high heat. Once the water reaches a boil, reduce the heat to maintain a gentle boil and set the timer for the required processing time. When the processing is complete, turn off the heat and remove the lid, tilting it away from you so that the steam won't burn your face and hands. Remove the jars with a jar lifter and place them on a towel with about 2 inches of space between them to cool. Allow the jars to cool completely at room temperature before checking for a seal, and do not touch the lid bands, as tightening or loosening them might interfere with the seal.

Test for a Seal: When the jars are cool, test the seal by pressing the center of the lid. It should not move or flex, but instead be completely concave. Remove the band and try gently prying off the lid with your finger. If the jars are not properly sealed, you can reprocess them within 24 hours to try to get a proper seal.

Experts recommend removing the lid bands on successfully sealed jars before storing, since bands can corrode or rust during storage. Label the sealed jars with their contents and the date they were canned and store in a cool, dark place. Once the jars are opened, they should be stored in the refrigerator. When you open a jar, make sure that the seal is still intact (lids should be difficult to pry off with a blunt edge or a bottle opener). Visually check for mold or other signs of deterioration and smell the contents to make sure there is no foul or unnatural odor. Store opened jars of food in the refrigerator and use within three weeks.

Condiments as Gifts

A homemade condiment in a beautiful jar or bottle makes a wonderful gift indeed. I've given batches of pickles, ketchups, and chutneys as gifts for holidays, teacher appreciation tokens, or hostess offerings.

Here are some tips on giving the homemade condiments in this book as gifts:

Give only small quantities, such as around 4 ounces, so that the recipient can use it all up before it goes bad. This applies particularly to foods that are not preserved by canning.

Seek out pretty jars or bottles. My favorite sources are:

Ball jars found in supermarkets, in gardening supply stores, and online. These classic jars come either plain or with a decorative quilted pattern embossed into the glass and include the classic, two-part lids. You can also sometimes find special limited-edition jars online (freshpreserving.com).

Williams-Sonoma offers gorgeous European-style glass jars with glass lids, as well as bottles with hinged stoppers. The store's website (williams-sonoma.com) also has a wide range of products to make your gifts even prettier, from paper and chalkboard tags, to decorative cords, to lid seals and personalized tag embossers.

Sunburst Bottle has every bottle shape, size, and color you can imagine. The company mostly sells to businesses but has no purchase minimums, so it's willing to work with consumers as well. The only catch is that you have to buy bottles by the case (typically 12 to 24, depending on the bottle or jar). Their website is sunburstbottle.com.

Leifheit Jars have a gorgeous, ornate shape and an embossed design. They're available through the company's website (leifheitus.com) or various other websites, including Sears and Amazon.com.

KitchenKrafts.com offers a variety of jars and bottles, from the classic Ball options to more commercial and specialized shapes and designs. There's even a mason jar with a mug handle!

Sur La Table has a wide range of canning equipment, jars, and bottles. It's a particularly good source for beautiful jars with decorative closures. Their website is surlatable.com.

Create an attractive label for your jars. Look for ready-made labels in craft stores or online, download templates from the Internet, or design your own on sticker paper or on regular paper that you can glue to the jar. Be sure to include what's inside, when it was made (or when it "expires"), and how to store it.

If all the important information doesn't fit on the label, include it on a pretty tag to tie to the jar with ribbon. You could list the ingredients or make serving suggestions, such as those included with each recipe in this book.

For greater impact, consider making the gift into a package or set. For instance, include a pretty spoon or spreader with mustards, some crackers with chutneys, a baguette with infused oils, or pound cake with dessert sauces.

Resources

Some of the recipes in this book contain specialty ingredients that might be hard to find in some parts of the country. These are some of my favorite sources for spices, specialty products, ethnic ingredients, equipment, and other items. Also be sure to check out the resources for decorative bottles and jars, page 120.

Asian Food Grocer
asianfoodgrocer.com
888-482-2742
A good source for Asian basics like soy sauce, rice vinegar, Asian spices, and wasabi.

Canning Pantry
canningpantry.com
800-285-9044
A wide selection of canning supplies, jars, and canning ingredients like pickling mix and canning salt.

New Mexico Catalog
newmexicocatalog.com
888-678-0585
Fresh or roasted green chiles shipped from New Mexico. Red chile pods and powder also available.

Penzey's Spices
penzeys.com
800-741-7787
One of the largest repertoires of spices and dried herbs, in 8-ounce and 1-pound bags as well as smaller quantities. An excellent source for mustard powder.

The Spice House
thespicehouse.com
847-328-3711
Excellent source for spices, dried herbs, vanilla extract, and chile powders.

Sur La Table
surlatable.com
800-243-0852
One of the most comprehensive sources for much of the equipment you'll need to make the recipes in this book, including cookware, cook's tools, scales, utensils, and food mills.

Conversion Charts

Volume Conversions

U.S.	U.S. Equivalent	Metric
1 tablespoon / 3 teaspoons	½ fluid ounce	15 ml
¼ cup	2 fluid ounces	60 ml
⅓ cup	3 fluid ounces	90 ml
½ cup	4 fluid ounces	120 ml
⅔ cup	5 fluid ounces	150 ml
¾ cup	6 fluid ounces	180 ml
1 cup	8 fluid ounces	240 ml
2 cups	16 fluid ounces	480 ml

Weight

U.S.	Metric
½ ounce	15 grams
1 ounce	30 grams
2 ounces	60 grams
¼ pound	115 grams
⅓ pound	150 grams
½ pound	225 grams
¾ pound	350 grams
1 pound	450 grams

Index

Condiment types (in **bold face**), recipe names, and major ingredients have been included in the index, although ubiquitous ingredients, such as olive oil or sugar, have not been indexed.

Aiolis, 35, 46–47
Almond Butter, 105
Almond oil, 105
Almonds, 94, 105, 106
Anchovies, 85, 92
Apple cider vinegar, 24, 25, 27, 37, 38, 41, 54, 59, 101
Apricot preserves, 91
Apricot Sweet and Sour Sauce, 91
Asian Quick Pickles, 52
Avocado Goddess Dressing, 84
Avocado-Tomatillo Salsa, 65
Avocados, 65, 84

Bacon, 101
Bacon fat, 43
Bacon Jam, 101
Bacon Mayonnaise, 43
Balsamic vinegar, 75
Barbecue sauces, 23, 24–26
Basic Mayonnaise, 42
Basil Aioli, 46
Beer, 37
Bell peppers, red: in aiolis, 47; in hot sauce, 58; in ketchups, 14–15; in relishes, 53, 54, 55; in specialty condiments, 95; in sweet sauces 30–31
Berries, frozen, 109
Berry Sauce, 109
Black Bean and Corn Salsa, 63
Black beans, 63
Blenders, 6
Blue Cheese Dressing, 86
Bourbon, 26

Bread and Butter Pickles, 51
Buttermilk, 80, 81, 84, 86

Caesar Dressing, 85
Canned foods, as staples, 4
Canning, 116–20; equipment, 117–18
Capered Tartar Sauce, 28
Capers, 28
Caramel Sauce, 108
Caramelized Onion Chutney, 98
Carrots, 52
Cashews, 115
Champagne, 38
Champagne-Dill Mustard, 38
Cherries, dried, 114
Cherry-Fig Compote, 114
Chile peppers: chipotle, 13, 45; green, 40, 62; habanero, 18, 58; jalapeño, 59, 60, 63, 64, 66, 90
Chimichurri, 93
Chipotle chile peppers, 13, 45
Chipotle Lime Mayonnaise, 45
Chocolate, 106, 110
Chocolate Almond Spread, 106
Chutneys, 98–100
Cider vinegar: in chutneys, 98, 99, 100; in ketchups, 10–11, 12, 14–15, 16–17; in mustards, 39; in relishes, 55
Cilantro, 64, 66, 94
Cilantro-Almond Pesto, 94
Classic Aioli, 46–47
Classic Ketchup from Canned Tomatoes, 12
Classic Tartar Sauce, 28
Classic Vinaigrette, 78

Cocktail Sauce, 33
Cocoa powder, 107
Coconut flakes, 115
Condensed milk, 111
Condiments: canning, 117–18; as gifts, 120–21; history, 2–3; kitchen equipment, 5–7. *See also specific types of condiments*
Conversion charts, 123
Cookware, 5
Corn, 53, 63
Corn and Pepper Relish, 53
Corn oil, 42–43, 44, 45
Corn syrup, 107, 108, 110, 112
Crunchy-Shell Chocolate Sauce, 110
Cubanelle, 58
Cucumbers: English, 52; pickling, 50, 51, 54, 55
Curried Ketchup, 20–21
Cutlery, 6
Cutting boards, 7

Daikon radishes, 52
Dijon Mayonnaise, 43
Dill, 80
Dill Pickles, 50
Dill Relish, 54
Dilly Horseradish Mayonnaise, 43
Dilly Ranch Dressing, 80
Disposable gloves, 7, 57
Dulce de Leche, 111

Eggs, 42–43, 44, 45, 46, 113
Equipment: canning, 117–18; kitchen, 5–7
Ethnic condiments, 89–93, 96–100
Evaporated milk, 107

Fig-Infused Vinegar, 73
Figs, dried, 73, 114
Food mills, 5
Food processors, 6

Food safety, and canning, 116–20
Fresh Tomato Ketchup, 10–11
Frozen foods, as staples, 4
Fruits, as staples, 4
Funnels, 6

Garlic, 70
Gifts, of condiments, 120–21
Ginger, 83, 100
Gloves, 7, 57
Grainy Porter Mustard, 37
Grana Padano cheese, 94
Grapeseed oil, 72, 83, 87, 94, 98, 104, 105, 106
Green Chile Mustard, 40
Green chile peppers, 40, 62
Green Chile Sauce, 62

Habanero chile peppers, 18, 58
Heavy cream, 108, 110
Herbed Balsamic Vinegar, 75
Herbs: dried, as staples, 3–4; fresh, as staples, 4
Hoisin Sauce, 97
Honey Mustard, 39
Horseradish, prepared, as ingredient, 33
Horseradish root, 32
Horseradish Sauce, 32
Hot Fudge Sauce, 107
Hot sauces, 57, 58–62. *See also* Salsas

Immersion blenders, 6
Infused oils, 69, 70–72
Italian parsley, 93

Jalapeño chile peppers: green, 59, 60, 63, 64, 66; red, 90
Jars, sterilizing, 118

Kalamata olives, 92
Ketchup, as ingredient, 24, 26, 33

Ketchups, 9, 10–21
Key Lime–Jalapeño Sauce, 60
Key lime juice, 60
Kitchen equipment, 5–7
Kitchen scales, 7
Knives, 6

Lemon Curd, 113
Lemon-Infused Oil, 72
Lemon Poppy Seed Buttermilk Dressing, 81
Lemons, 72; juice, 81, 84, 85, 113; zest, 46–47, 113
Lemony Aioli, 46–47
Lime-Cumin Dressing, 82
Lime juice, 82
Liquor: bourbon, 26; sherry, 96; whiskey, 26; wine, 30–31, 38, 114
Luscious Lemon Curd, 113

Mango Chutney, 100
Mangoes, 100; cutting, 67; dried, 66
Maple syrup, 79, 112
Maple Tarragon Vinaigrette, 79
Mayonnaise, as ingredient, 28, 29, 80, 84, 86
Mayonnaises, 35, 42–47
Measurement conversions, 123
Measuring utensils, 6
Milk, 106; condensed, 111; evaporated, 107
Mirin (Japanese wine), 96
Miso paste, 87, 97
Mixing bowls, 5
Molasses, 24, 25, 97
Mom's Red Chile Sauce, 61
Mustard, as ingredient, 25
Mustard-Based Barbecue Sauce, 25
Mustard powder, 36, 39, 40, 41, 42–43, 82
Mustard seeds, 37, 38, 41, 51, 100
Mustards, 35, 36–41

Oils, infused, 69, 70–72
Olives, kalamata, 92
Onions: in barbecue sauces, 24, 26; in chutneys, 98, 99, 100; in hot sauces, 62; in ketchups, 10–11, 12, 13, 18; in mustards, 41; in pickles, 51; in relishes, 53, 55; in specialty condiments, 101
Onions, green, 52
Onions, red, 64
Orange juice, 87
Orange-Miso Dressing, 87

Pantry staples, 3–4
Parsley, Italian, 93
Peanut Butter, 104
Peanut oil, 104
Peanuts, 104
Pear Chutney, 99
Pears, 99
Pickle crisp, 50, 51
Pickles, 49, 50–52
Pickles, dill, 28
Pico de Gallo, 64
Pineapples, 66, 115; cutting, 67
Pinot noir, 114
Prepared Horseradish Sauce, 32

Raisins, 27, 98, 99, 100
Raspberries, 74
Raspberry Vinegar, 74
Red bell peppers. *See* Bell peppers, red
Red Chile Sauce, 61
Red Pepper Coulis, 30–31
Red Pepper Preserves, 95
Red wine vinegar, 20–21, 78, 86, 93
Relishes, 49, 53–55
Remoulade, 29
Rice vinegar, 19, 52, 87, 91, 96, 97
Roasted Garlic Olive Oil, 70

Roasted Red Pepper Aioli, 47
Romano cheese, 94
Rooster-Style Sauce, 59
Rosemary, 71
Rosemary-Infused Oil, 71

Salad dressings, 77, 78–87
Salsas, 57, 63–66
Sauces, 23, 27–33; hot, 57, 58–62; sweet, 103, 107–15
Scales, 7
Sesame-Ginger Dressing, 83
Sesame oil, 83, 97
Shallots, 16–17, 20, 30, 81
Sherry, 96
Smoked Tomato Ketchup, 16–17
Sour cream, 80
Southwestern Tomatillo Ketchup, 19
Soy sauce, 96, 97
Specialty condiments, 89, 94–95, 101
Spices, as staples, 3–4
Spicy Chipotle Ketchup, 13
Spicy Habanero Ketchup, 18
Spicy Smooth Mustard, 36
Spreads, 103, 104–106
Staples, 3–4
Steak Sauce, 27
Sun-Dried Tomato Mayonnaise, 44
Sweet Chili Sauce, 90
Sweet Pickle Relish, 55
Sweet sauces, 103, 107–15

Tangy Two-Pepper Sauce, 58
Tapenade, 92
Tarragon, 43, 79
Tarragon Mayonnaise, 43
Tartar Sauce, 28

Tasting spoons, 7
Teriyaki Sauce, 96
Thyme, 75
Tomatillos, 19, 65
Tomato-Based Barbecue Sauce, 24
Tomato paste, 27
Tomato–Roasted Red Pepper Ketchup, 14–15
Tomatoes: in ketchups, 10–21; in salsas, 63, 64
Tomatoes, sun-dried, 44
Tropical Pineapple-Cashew Compote, 115
Tropical Salsa, 66

Vegetable oil, 42–43, 61, 62, 87, 106
Vegetables, as staples, 4
Vidalia Mustard, 41
Vinaigrettes, 77, 78–79
Vinegar, as ingredient. *See specific types* (balsamic, wine, *etc.*)
Vinegars, 69, 73–75
Vinegars, as staples, 3

Walnuts, 112
Wet Walnuts, 112
Whiskey, 26
Whiskey-Spiked Barbecue Sauce, 26
Whisks, 5
White vinegar: in ethnic condiments, 90, 100; in hot sauces, 58, 60; in ketchups, 13, 14–15; in mayonnaises, 42–43, 44, 45; in pickles, 50, 51, 53; in sauces, 27, 32; in specialty condiments, 95
White wine vinegar, 36, 40, 73, 74, 79
Wine: champagne, 38; pinot noir, 114; white, 30–31
Wine vinegars: red, 20–21, 78, 86, 93; white, 36, 40, 73, 74, 79

Yogurt, 85

About the Author

JESSICA HARLAN has written about food and cooking for nearly two decades. A graduate of the Institute of Culinary Education, she has developed recipes for well-known food brands, toured olive oil and pasta factories in Italy, reported on the newest food trends at industry trade shows across the country, judged food competitions, interviewed celebrity chefs, catered swanky Manhattan cocktail parties, and taught cooking classes.

She has written for *Clean Eating* magazine, *Gentle Kitchen*, *Time Out New York Eating and Drinking Guide*, *Town and Country*, *Pilates Style*, *Mobile Travel Guide Atlanta*, About.com, and Gaiam.com. This is her fourth cookbook. The previous books, all published by Ulysses Press, include *Ramen to the Rescue*, *Quinoa Cuisine* (co-written with Kelley Sparwasser), and *Tortillas to the Rescue*.

She lives in Atlanta, Georgia, with her husband and two daughters.